QUOTAT
BOOK

PENTAGON PRESS
DELHI INDIA

QUOTATIONS BOOK

First Published : 2004
Reprinted 2005

ISBN 81 86830 29 4

Published by :
PENTAGON PRESS
A-38, Hauz Khas,
New Delhi-110016
Ph.: 011-51517091, 51656996,7,8
INDIA

Printed at :
Print Perfect
C-209/1, Mayapuri II
New Delhi 110 064

PREFACE

'Pentagon's Quotation Book' is an accumulation of numerous quotations on various issues, topics and subjects from the most illustrious authors, writers, poets, philosophers, ideologists etc.

The Book has some of the most famous and breathtaking phrases from the eternal plays of Shakespeare. It also consists some of the most popular ideologies of great thinkers like Oscar Wilde, Plato and Sigmund Freud. The famous quotations from the works of great authors like Mark Twain, Charles Dickens, Jane Austen, Mark Twain and William Blake have also been included.

The Book is classified as per topics and consists of many diverse themes and spell bounding quotations. The sayings and writings on themes such as *War, Peace* and *Optimism and Pessimism* are the highlight of the book. It consists of some of the most amazing inspirational quotations on topics like *Adversity, Beauty* and *Death* etc.

Quotations on philosophical topics such as *Life* and *Love* have also been provided in the Book. It also has some of the most humorous quotations on *Joy* and *Laughter*. It provides an ample opportunity for a person to see beyond the realities of life and read some of the facts that seem to be simple but are not realised by the humans at times.

Overall, a bank of the wealthiest of sayings and writings, 'Pentagon's Quotation Book' is a great collection of the most intriguing quotations from the past and the present, surely to be loved by the old and child alike.

ABSENCE

Absence makes the heart grow fonder,
Isle of Beauty. Fare thee well!

—Thomas H. Bayly, *Isle of Beauty*

ACCIDENTS

Accidents will occur in the best—regulated families; and in families not regulated by that pervading influence which sanctifies while it enhances the—a—I would say, in short, by the influence of Woman, in the lofty character of Wife …

—Dickens, *David Copperfield*

ACCOMPLISHMENT

The road to success is filled with women pushing their husbands along.

—Attributed to Lord Thomas R. Dewar

I have climbed to the top of the greasy pole!

—Benjamin Disraeli

The secret of success is constancy of purpose.

—Benjamin Disraeli

If a man can write a better book, preach a better sermon, or make a better mousetrap than his neighbor, … the world will make a beaten path to his door.

—Attributed to Ralph Waldo Emerson

But I like not these great successes of yours; for I know how jealous are the gods.

—Herodotus

Even on the most exalted throne in the world we are only sitting on our own bottom.

—Michel Eyquem de Montaigne

There is only one success ... to be able to spend your life in your own way, and not to give others absurd maddening claims upon it.

—Christopher Morley

ADMINISTRATION

No rule is so general,
which admits not some exception.

—Robert Burton

The general rule, at least, is that while property may be regulated to a certain extent, if regulation goes too far it will be recognized as a taking.

—Oliver Wendell Holmes

It is hardly lack of due process for the Government to regulate that which it subsidizes.

—Robert H. Jackson

Every system should allow loopholes and exceptions, for if it does not, it will in the end crush all that is best in man.

—Bertrand Russell

Will one of you gentlemen tell me in what civilized country of the earth there are important government boards of control on which private interests are represented? Which of you gentlemen thinks the railroads should select members of the Interstate Commerce Commission?

—Attributed to Woodrow Wilson

ADVERSITY

Sweet are the uses of adversity;
Which, like the toad, ugly and venomous,
Wears yet a precious jewel in his head,

—Shakespeare, As You *Like It, II, I 1*

There is no ghost so difficult to lay as the ghost of an injury.

—Alexander Smith

Despair is anger with no place to go.

—Mignon McLaughlin, *The Neurotic's Notebook*, 1960

In a real dark night of the soul, it is always three o'clock in the morning, day after day.

—F. Scott Fitzgerald

Problems are messages.

—Shakti Gawain

There is in every true woman's heart, a spark of heavenly fire, which lies dormant in the broad daylight of prosperity; but which kindles up, and beams and blazes in the dark hour of adversity.

—Washington Irving, *The Sketch Book*, 1820

For fate has wove the thread of life with pain,
And twins ev'n from the birth are Misery and Man!

—Homer, *Odyssey*

To have become a deeper man is the privilege of those who have suffered.

—Oscar Wilde

The art of living lies less in eliminating our troubles than in growing with them.

—Bernard M. Baruch

Doing what's right is no guarantee against misfortune.

—William McFee

A new wound makes all the old ones ache again.

—Mignon McLaughlin, *The Neurotic's Notebook*, 1960

The turning point in the process of growing up is when you discover the core of strength within you that survives all hurt.

—Max Lerner, *The Unfinished Country*, 1950

God uses suffering as a whetstone, to make men sharp with.

—Henry Ward Beecher

Hardship is best sailed with a heart ship.

—Tas Soft Wind

Real pain can alone cure us of imaginary ills. We feel a thousand miseries till we are lucky enough to feel misery.

—Samuel Taylor Coleridge

Everybody ought to do at least two things each day that he hates to do, just for practice.

—William James

He that struggles with us strengthens our nerves, and sharpens our skill. Our antagonist is our helper.

—Edmund Burke, *The Revolution in France*, 1790

The course of true anything never does run smooth.

—Samuel Butler

Nothing prevents happiness like the memory of happiness.

—André Gide, *L'immoraliste*

If the thunder is not loud, the peasant forgets to cross himself.

—Russian Proverb

Past and to come, seems best; things present, worse.

—William Shakespeare, *Henry IV*

People don't ever seem to relate that doing what's right is no guarantee against misfortune.

—William McFee, *Casuals of the Sea*, 1916

Better to lose count while naming your blessings than to lose your blessings to counting your troubles.

—Maltbie D. Babcock

Every evil is some good spelt backwards, and in it the wise know how to read Wisdom.

—Coventry Patmore

May you get what you wish for.

—Old Chinese Curse

You'll never find a better sparring partner than adversity.

—Walt Schmidt

Watch a man in times of … adversity to discover what kind of man he is; for then at last words of truth are drawn from the depths of his heart, and the mask is torn off.

—Lucretius, *On the Nature of Things*

"The horror of that moment," the King went on, "I shall never, never forget!" "You will, though," the Queen said, "if you don't make a memorandum of it.

—Lewis Carroll, *Through the Looking Glass*, 1872

Perhaps everything terrible is in its deepest being something helpless that wants help from us.

—Rainer Maria Rilke

If we will be quiet and ready enough, we shall find compensation in every disappointment.

—Henry David Thoreau

There are times in everyone's life when something constructive is born out of adversity ... when things seem so bad that you've got to grab your fate by the shoulders and shake it.

—Author Unknown

Prosperity is not without many fears and distastes, and adversity is not without comforts and hopes.

—Francis Bacon

The trouble with most of us is that we would rather be ruined by praise than saved by criticism.

—Norman Vincent Peale

It is better to drink of deep griefs than to taste shallow pleasures.

—William Hazlitt, *Characteristics*, 1823

Problems are only opportunities with thorns on them.

—Hugh Miller, *Snow on the Wind*

The darkest hour has only sixty minutes.

—Morris Mandel

God gave burdens, also shoulders.

—Yiddish Proverb

There is something beautiful about all scars of whatever nature. A scar means the hurt is over, the wound is closed and healed, done with.

—Harry Crews

When suffering comes, we yearn for some sign from God, forgetting we have just had one.

—Mignon McLaughlin, *The Neurotic's Notebook*, 1960

Man performs and engenders so much more than he can or should have to bear. That's how he finds that he can bear anything.

—William Faulkner

We shall draw from the heart of suffering itself the means of inspiration and survival.

—Winston Churchill

My strength is made perfect in weakness.

—II Corinthians

Problems are the price you pay for progress.

—Branch Rickey

When you're feeling your worst, that's when you get to know yourself the best.

—Leslie Grossman

Happiness is beneficial for the body, but it is grief that develops the powers of the mind.

—Marcel Proust, *The Past Recaptured, Remembrance of Things Past*

Your most unhappy customers are your greatest source of learning.

—Bill Gates, *Business @ the Speed of Thought*

The art of living lies less in eliminating our troubles than in growing with them.

—Bernard M. Baruch

Like a plant that starts up in showers and sunshine and does not know which has best helped it to grow, it is difficult to say whether the hard things or the pleasant things did me the most good.

—Lucy Larcom

If all misfortunes were laid in one common heap whence everyone must take an equal portion, most people would be contented to take their own and depart.

—Socrates

Men grow tired of sleep, love, singing and dancing sooner than of war.

—Homer, *Iliad*

There's nothing that cleanses your soul like getting the hell kicked out of you.

—Woody Hayes

It is foolish to tear one's hair in grief, as though sorrow would be made less by baldness.

—Cicero

Failure is the condiment that gives success its flavor.

—Truman Capote

No man ought to lay a cross upon himself, or to adopt tribulation, as is done in popedom; but if a cross or tribulation come upon him, then let him suffer it patiently, and know that it is good and profitable for him.

—Martin Luther

Having is not so pleasing a thing as wanting, it may not be logical but it is often true.

—Mr. Spock, *Star Trek*

I have woven a parachute out of everything broken.

—William Stafford

I have heard there are troubles of more than one kind.
Some come from ahead and some come from behind.
But I've bought a big bat. I'm all ready you see.

Now my troubles are going to have troubles with me!

—Dr. Seuss

The misfortunes of mankind are of varied plumage.

—Aeschylus, *The Suppliant Maidens*

To be without some of the things you want is an indispensable part of happiness.

—Bertrand Russell

Mishaps are like knives, that either serve us or cut us, as we grasp them by the blade or the handle.

—James Russell Lowell, "Cambridge Thirty Years Ago," *Literary Essays*

Criticism may not be agreeable, but it is necessary. It fulfils the same function as pain in the human body. It calls attention to an unhealthy state of things.

—Winston Churchill

If the wind will not serve, take to the oars.

—Latin Proverb

We look before and after,
And pine for what is not;
Our sincerest laughter
With some pain is fraught;
Our sweetest songs are those that tell of saddest thought.

—Percy Bysshe Shelley, "Ode to a Sky Lark"

In this world there are only two tragedies. One is not getting what one wants, and the other is getting it.

—Oscar Wilde, *Lady Windemere's Fan*, 1896

Count the garden by the flowers, never by the leaves that fall. Count your life with smiles and not the tears that roll.

—Author Unknown

Poverty, frost, famine, rain, disease, are the beadles and guardsmen that hold us to Common Sense.

—Ralph Waldo Emerson

Adversity has the same effect on a man that severe training has on the pugilist: it reduces him to his fighting weight.

—Josh Billings

In our nature, however, there is a provision, alike marvelous and merciful, that the sufferer should never know the intensity of what he endures by its present torture, but chiefly by the pang that rankles after it.

—Nathaniel Hawthorne

Every rose has its thorn.

—Author Unknown

You never know what you've got until it's gone.

—Author Unknown

That was rough.... Thing to do now is try and forget it.... I guess I don't quite mean that. It's not a thing you can forget. Maybe not even a thing you want to forget.... Life's like that sometimes ... Now and then for no good reason a man can figure out, life will just haul off and knock him flat, slam him agin' the ground so hard it seems like all his insides is busted. But it's not all like that. A lot of it's mighty fine, and you can't afford to waste the good part frettin' about the bad. That makes it all bad.... Sure, I know — sayin' it's one thing and feelin' it's another. But I'll tell you a trick that's sometimes a big help. When you start lookin' around for something good to take the place of the bad, as a general rule you can find it.

—From the movie *Old Yeller*

God brings men into deep waters not to drown them, but to cleanse them.

—Aughey

Let me embrace thee, sour adversity, for wise men say it is the wisest course.

—William Shakespeare

There are two things that one must get used to or one will find life unendurable: the damages of time and injustices of men.

—Nicolas Chamfort

AMBITION

All ambitions are lawful except those which climb upward on the miseries or credulities of mankind.

—Joseph Conrad, A *Personal Record*

I would rather be the first man here than the second in Rome.

—Julius Caesar (according to Plutarch)

I had Ambition, by which sin
The angels fell;
I climbed and, step by step. O Lord,
Ascended into Hell.

—W. H. Davies, Ambition

ANGER

I was angry with my friend;
I told my wrath, my wrath did end.
I was angry with my foe;
I told it not, my wrath did grow.

—William Blake, A Poison Tree

ATTITUDE

A positive attitude may not solve all your problems, but it will annoy enough people to make it worth the effort.

—Herm Albright, quoted in *Reader's Digest*, June 1995

Attitudes are contagious. Is yours worth catching?

—Author Unknown

Wherever you go, no matter what the weather, always bring your own sunshine.

—Anthony J. D'Angelo, *The College Blue Book*

If you don't get everything you want, think of the things you don't get that you don't want.

—Oscar Wilde

I had the blues because I had no shoes until upon the street, I met a man who had no feet.

—Ancient Persian Saying

If you don't think every day is a good day, just try missing one.

—Cavett Robert

It's so hard when I have to, and so easy when I want to.

—Annie Gottlier

Oh, my friend, it's not what they take away from you that counts. It's what you do with what you have left.

—Hubert Humphrey

Attitude is a little thing that makes a big difference.

—Winston Churchill

Every day may not be good, but there's something good in every day.

—Author Unknown

The sun shines and warms and lights us and we have no curiosity to know why this is so; but we ask the reason of all evil, of pain, and hunger, and mosquitoes and silly people.

—Ralph Waldo Emerson

To be interested in the changing seasons is a happier state of mind than to be hopelessly in love with spring.

—George Santayana

Happiness is an attitude. We either make ourselves miserable, or happy and strong. The amount of work is the same.

—Francesca Reigler

If you don't like something change it; if you can't change it, change the way you think about it.

—Mary Engelbreit

So often time it happens, we all live our life in chains, and we never even know we have the key.

—The Eagles, "Already Gone"

The only people who find what they are looking for in life are the fault finders.

—Foster's Law

He who has so little knowledge of human nature as to seek happiness by changing anything but his own disposition will waste his life in fruitless efforts.

—Samuel Johnson

Think big thoughts but relish small pleasures.

—H. Jackson Brown, Jr., *Life's Little Instruction Book*

Every thought is a seed. If you plant crab apples, don't count on harvesting Golden Delicious.

—Bill Meyer

We are all in the gutter, but some of us are looking at the stars.

—Oscar Wilde, *Lady Windermere's Fan*, 1893

Blessed is he who expects nothing, for he shall never be disappointed.

—Attributed to both Jonathan Swift and Benjamin Franklin

To be upset over what you don't have is to waste what you do have.

—Ken S. Keyes, Jr., *Handbook to Higher Consciousness*

The only disability in life is a bad attitude.

—Scott Hamilton

If you aren't fired with enthusiasm, you will be fired with enthusiasm.

—Vince Lombardi

My riches consist not in the extent of my possessions, but in the fewness of my wants.

—J. Brotherton

There is nothing so easy but that it becomes difficult, when you do it reluctantly.

—Publius Terentius Afer

I don't like that man. I must get to know him better.

—Abraham Lincoln

Just because you're miserable doesn't mean you can't enjoy your life.

—Annette Goodheart

In the depth of winter I finally learned that there was in me an invincible summer.

—Albert Camus, *Lyrical and Critical Essays*

Let us rise up and be thankful, for if we didn't learn a lot today, at least we learned a little, and if we didn't learn a little, at least we didn't get sick, and if we got sick, at least we didn't die; so, let us all be thankful.

—Buddha

There are no menial jobs, only menial attitudes.

—William J. Bennett, *The Book of Virtues*

I always plucked a thistle and planted a flower where I thought a flower would grow.

—Abraham Lincoln

Got no checkbooks, got no banks,

Still I'd like to express my thanks —

I got the sun in the morning and the moon at night.

—Irving Berlin, "I Got the Sun in the Morning," 1946

To everyone is given the key to heaven; the same key opens the gates of hell.

—Ancient Proverb

True contentment depends not upon what we have; a tub was large enough for Diogenes, but a world was too little for Alexander.

—Charles Caleb Colton

To be wronged is nothing unless you continue to remember it.

—Confucius

I don't think of all the misery but of the beauty that still remains.

—Anne Frank, *The Diary of a Young Girl*

The best things in life are unexpected — because there were no expectations.

—Eli Khamarov, *Surviving on Planet Reebok*

Affectation is a greater enemy to the face than smallpox.

—English Proverb

Say you are well, or all is well with you,
And God shall hear your words and make them true.

—Ella Wheeler Wilcox

A person will sometimes devote all his life to the development of one part of his body — the wishbone.

—Robert Frost

If we shall take the good we find, asking no questions, we shall have heaping measures.

—Ralph Waldo Emerson

The greatest discovery of my generation is that a human being can alter his life by altering his attitudes.

—William James

Nothing contributes so much to tranquilize the mind as a steady purpose — a point on which the soul may fix its intellectual eye.

—Mary Wollstonecraft Shelley, *Frankenstein*, 1818

When you feel dog tired at night, it may be because you've growled all day long.

—Author Unknown

Could we change our attitude, we should not only see life differently, but life itself would come to be different.

—Katherine Mansfield

Enjoy the little things, for one day you may look back and realize they were the big things.

—Robert Brault

Let me enjoy the earth no less
Because the all—enacting Might
Which fashioned forth its loveliness
Had other aims than my delight.

—Thomas Hardy, *Time's Laughingstocks and Other Verses*, 1909

Whenever you fall, pick something up.

—Oswald Avery

Success is due less to ability than to zeal.

—Charles Buxton

My father's nature turned out no waste product; he had none of that useless stuff in him that lies in heaps near factories. He took his own happiness with him.

—Margot Asquith

We awaken in others the same attitude of mind we hold toward them.

—Elbert Hubbard

If my resolution to be a great man was half so strong as it is to despise the shame of being a little one ...

—William Cowper

I think, what has this day brought me, and what have I given it?

—Henry Moore

My pain is self – chosen.

—Mad Season, "River of Deceit"

I am an optimist. It does not seem too much use being anything else.

—Winston Churchill

What counts is not necessarily the size of the dog in the fight — it's the size of the fight in the dog.

—Dwight Eisenhower, address to Republican National Committee, 31 January 1958

Look at everything as though you were seeing it either for the first or last time.

—Betty Smith

Henceforth, I ask not good—fortune, I myself am good—fortune.

—Walt Whitman

No life is so hard that you can't make it easier but it is the way you take it.

—Ellen Glasgow

I have learned to use the word impossible with the greatest caution.

—Wernher von Braun

There's a saying among prospectors: 'Go out looking for one thing, and that's all you'll ever find.'

—Robert Flaherty

The human spirit is stronger than anything that can happen to it.

—C.C. Scott

I am a little deaf, a little blind, a little impotent, and on top of this are two or three abominable infirmities, but nothing destroys my hope.

—Voltaire

The excursion is the same when you go looking for your sorrow as when you go looking for your joy.

—Eudora Welty

Being a sex symbol has to do with an attitude, not looks. Most men think it's looks, most women know otherwise.

—Kathleen Turner

Too many people miss the silver lining, because they're expecting gold.

—Maurice Setter

We cannot direct the wind, but we can adjust the sails.

—Author Unknown

Misery is a communicable disease.

—Martha Graham

If you have the will to win, you have achieved half your success; if you don't, you have achieved half your failure.

—David Ambrose

If the skies fall, one may hope to catch larks.

—Francis Rabelais

A happy person is not a person in a certain set of circumstances, but rather a person with a certain set of attitudes.

—Hugh Downs

Very often a change of self is needed more than a change of scene.

—Arthur Christopher Benson

Some people are always grumbling because roses have thorns; I am thankful that thorns have roses.

—Alphonse Karr

If you call a thing bad you do little, if you call a thing good you do much.

—Johann Wolfgang von Goethe

The Kingdom of Heaven is not a place, but a state of mind.

—John Burroughs

Since the house is on fire let us warm ourselves.

—Italian Proverb

Reach for the stars, even if you have to stand on a cactus.

—Susan Longacre

I not only bow to the inevitable; I am fortified by it.

—Thornton Wilder

I never really look for anything. What God throws my way comes. I wake up in the morning and whichever way God turns my feet, I go.

—Pearl Bailey

Men who never get carried away should be.

—Malcolm Forbes

Become a possibilitarian. No matter how dark things seem to be or actually are, raise your sights and see possibilities — always see them, for they're always there.

—Norman Vincent Peale

Surrounded by people who love life, you love it too; surrounded by people who don't, you don't.

—Mignon McLaughlin, *The Second Neurotic's Notebook*, 1966

Physical strength is measured by what we can carry; spiritual by what we can bear.

—Author Unknown

We can destroy ourselves by cynicism and disillusion, just as effectively as by bombs.

—Kenneth Clark

The impossible can always be broken down into possibilities.

—Author Unknown

Without enthusiasm, virtue functions not at all, and vice only poorly.

—Mignon McLaughlin, *The Neurotic's Notebook*, 1960

I am sure that nothing has such a decisive influence upon a man's course as his personal appearance, and not so much his appearance as his belief in its attractiveness or unattractiveness.

—Leo Tolstoy

Be enthusiastic. Remember the placebo effect — 30% of medicine is showbiz.

—Ronald Spark

It is no use to grumble and complain;
It's just as cheap and easy to rejoice;
When God sorts out the weather and
sends rain —Why, rain's my choice.

—James Whitcomb Riley

Impossible is a word only to be found in the dictionary of fools.

—Napoleon

Things turn out best for the people who make the best out of the way things turn out.

—Art Linkletter

I have never met a man so ignorant that I couldn't learn something from him.

—Galileo Galilei

Heaven is under our feet, as well as over our heads.

—Henry David Thoreau

A loving person lives in a loving world. A hostile person lives in a hostile world; everyone you meet is your mirror.

—Ken Keyes, Jr.

Is life so wretched? Isn't it rather your hands, which are too small, your vision that is muddled? You are the one who must grow up.

—Dag Hammarskjold

People are not disturbed by things, but by the view they take of them.

—Epictetus

Swallow a toad in the morning and you will encounter nothing more disgusting the rest of the day.

—Nicholas Chamfort

A cloudy day is no match for a sunny disposition.

—William Arthur Ward

BEAUTY

What is lovely never dies,
But passes into other loveliness.

—Thomas Bailey Aldrich, A *Shadow of the light*

There is no excellent beauty that hath not some strangeness in the proportion.

—Francis Bacon, *Essays: Of Beauty*

If you get simple beauty and naught else,
You get about the best thing God invents.

—R. Browning, Fra Lippo Lippi

She walks in beauty, like the night
Of cloudless climes and starry skies;
And all that's best of dark and bright
Meet in her aspect and her eyes;

—Byron. *She Walks in Beauty*

Lord of the far horizons,
Give us the eyes to see
Over the verge of the sundown
The beauty that is to be.

—Bliss Carman, *Lord of the Far Horizons*

She is not fair to outward view
As many maidens be:
Her loveliness I never knew
Until she smiled on me:

—Hartley Coleridge, Song

I slept and dreamed that life was beauty.
I woke—and found that life was duty:
Was my dream, then, a shadowy lie?
Toil on, sad heart, courageously,
And thou shalt find thy dream shall be
A noonday light and truth to thee.

—Ellen Sturgis Hooper, *Beauty and Duty*

Beauty for some provides escape.
Who gain a happiness in eyeing
The gorgeous buttocks of the ape

Or autumn sunsets exquisitely dying.

—Aldous Huxley, *The Ninth Philosopher's Song*

The beauty of things was born before eyes and
sufficient to itself, the heart—breaking beauty
Will remain when there is no heart to break for it.

—Robinson Jeffers, *Credo*

A thing of beauty is a Joy for ever:
Its loveliness increases: it will never
Pass into nothingness

—Keats. *Endymion*

"Beauty is truth, truth beauty,"— that is all
Ye know on earth, and all ye need to know.

—Keats. *Ode on a Grecian Urn*

Beauty is that Medusa's head
Which men go armed to seek and sever.
It is most deadly when most dead,
And dead will stare and sting forever.

—Archibald Macleish, *Beauty*

Beauty is Nature's coin, must not be hoarded,
But must be current, and the good thereof
Consists in mutual and partaken bliss ...

—Milton, *Cornus*

As the lily among thorns, so is my love among the daughters.

—Old Testament, *Song of Solomon, II, 2*

Beauty is excrescence, superabundance. random ebullience, and sheer delightful waste to be enjoyed in its own high right.

—Donald Culross Peattie, *An Almanac for Moderns*

Helen, thy beauty is to me
Like those Nicaean barks of yore,
That gently o'er a perfumed sea,
The weary, wayworn wanderer bore
To his own native shore.

—Poe. *To Helen*

She was good as she was fair,
None, none on earth above her!
As pure in thought as angels are:
To know her was to love her.

—Samuel Rogers, *Jacqueline*

Remember that the most beautiful things in the world are the most useless; peacocks and lilies, for example.

—John Ruskin, The Stones of Venice, I

Though we travel the world over to find the beautiful, we must carry it with us or we find it not.

—Ralph Waldo Emerson

Our hearts are drunk with a beauty our eyes could never see.

—George W. Russell

I've never seen a smiling face that was not beautiful.

—Author Unknown

Against Him those women sin who torment their skin with potions, stain their cheeks with rouge and extend the line of their eyes with black coloring. Doubtless they are dissatisfied with God's plastic skill. In their own persons they convict and censure the Artificer of all things.

—Tertullian

That which is striking and beautiful is not always good, but that which is good is always beautiful.

—Ninon de L'Enclos

Had the price of looking been blindness, I would have looked.

—Ralph Ellison, *"Battle Royal"*

Some people, no matter how old they get, never lose their beauty — they merely move it from their faces into their hearts.

—Martin Buxbaum

Tell them dear, that if eyes were made for seeing,
Then beauty is its own excuse for being

—Ralph Waldo Emerson, *"The Rhodora"*

It is amazing how complete is the delusion that beauty is goodness.

—Leo Tolstoy

In every man's heart there is a secret nerve that answers to the vibrations of beauty.

—Christopher Morley

What humbugs we are, who pretend to live for Beauty, and never see the Dawn!

—Logan Pearsall Smith

The most beautiful view is the one I share with you.

—Author Unknown

When you have only two pennies left in the world, buy a loaf of bread with one, and a lily with the other.

—Chinese Proverb

Beauty comes in all sizes, not just size 5.

—Roseanne

There is a road from the eye to the heart that does not go through the intellect.

—Gilbert Keith Chesterton

We ascribe beauty to that which is simple; which has no superfluous parts; which exactly answers its end; which stands related to all things; which is the mean of many extremes.

—Ralph Waldo Emerson

Everything has beauty, but not everyone sees it.

—Confucius

Plainness has its peculiar temptations quite as much as beauty.

—George Eliot

As we grow old, the beauty steals inward.

—Ralph Waldo Emerson

The soul that sees beauty may sometimes walk alone.

—Johann von Goethe

A woman who cannot be ugly is not beautiful.

—Karl Kraus

Beauty deprived of its proper foils and adjuncts ceases to be enjoyed as beauty, just as light deprived of all shadows ceases to be enjoyed as light.

—John Ruskin

Beauty in the flesh will continue to rule the world.

—Florenz Ziegfeld

You don't love a woman because she is beautiful, she is beautiful because you love her.

—Author Unknown

One summer night, out on a flat headland, all but surrounded by the waters of the bay, the horizons were remote and distant rims on the edge of space. Millions of stars blazed in darkness, and on the far shore a few lights burned in cottages. Otherwise there was no reminder of human life. My companion and I were alone with the stars: the misty river of the Milky Way flowing across the sky, the patterns of the constellations standing out bright and clear, a blazing planet low on the horizon. It occurred to me that if this were a sight that could be seen only once in a century, this little headland would be thronged with spectators. But it can be see many scores of nights in any year, and so the lights burned in the cottages and the inhabitants probably gave not a thought to the beauty overhead; and because they could see it almost any night, perhaps they never will.

—Rachel Carson

Flowers ... are a proud assertion that a ray of beauty outvalues all the utilities of the world.

—Ralph Waldo Emerson, 1844

A morning glory at my window satisfies me more than the metaphysics of books.

—Walt Whitman

Beauty ... is the shadow of God on the universe.

—Gabriela Mistral, *Desolacíon*

One may have a blazing hearth in one's soul and yet no one ever comes to sit by it. Passers by see only a wisp of smoke from the chimney and continue on the way.

—Vincent Van Gogh

Beauty? ... To me it is a word without sense because I do not know where its meaning comes from nor where it leads to.

—Pablo Picasso

You can take no credit for beauty at sixteen. But if you are beautiful at sixty, it will be your soul's own doing.

—Marie Stopes

I'm tired of all this nonsense about beauty being only skin deep. That's deep enough. What do you want — an adorable pancreas?

—Jean Kerr, *The Snake Has All the Lines*

Beauty is indeed a good gift of God; but that the good may not think it a great good, God dispenses it even to the wicked.

—Saint Augustine

Taking joy in living is a woman's best cosmetic.

—Rosalind Russell

I hope you have lost your good looks, for while they last any fool can adore you, and the adoration of fools is bad for the soul. No, give me a ruined complexion and a lost figure and sixteen chins on a farmyard of Crow's feet and an obvious wig. Then you shall see me coming out strong.

—George Bernard Shaw, to Mrs. Patrick Campbell

Beauty isn't worth thinking about; what's important is your mind. You don't want a fifty—dollar haircut on a fifty—cent head.

—Garrison Keillor

BONDAGE

But this is slavery, not to speak one's thought.

—Euripides

Whenever [I] hear any one arguing for slavery I feel a strong impulse to see it tried on him personally.

—Abraham Lincoln

All socialism involves slavery ... That which fundamentally distinguishes the slave is that he labours under coercion to satisfy another's desires.

—Herbert Spencer

CALMNESS

In some causes silence is dangerous; so if any know of conspiracies against their country or king, or any that might greatly prejudice their neighbor, they ought to discover it.

—Attributed to St. Ambrose

Under all speech that is good for anything there lies a silence that is better. Silence is deep as Eternity; speech is shallow as Time.

—Thomas Carlyle

Blessed is the man who, having nothing to say, abstains from giving us wordy evidence of the fact.

—George Eliot

We will have to repent in this generation not merely for the vitriolic words and actions of the bad people, but for the appalling silence of the good people.

—Martin Luther King, Jr.

Silence is the perfectest herald of joy:
I were but little happy if I could say how much.

—Shakespeare

CAUSE

A crowd always thinks with its sympathy, never with its reason.

—William Alger

Ethics make one's soul mannerly and wise, but logic is the armory of reason, furnished with all offensive and defensive weapons.

—Thomas Fuller

A man always has two reasons for what he does—a good one, and the real one.

—Attributed to J. Pierpont Morgan

CLIMATE

For the man sound in body and serene of mind there is no such thing as bad weather! every sky has its beauty, and storms which whip the blood do but make it pulse more vigorously.

—George Gissing

We may achieve climate, but weather is thrust upon us.

—O. Henry

Climate is theory. Weather is condition.

—Oliver Herford

I wonder that any human being should remain in a cold country who could find room in a warm one.

—Thomas Jefferson

When it is evening, ye say, it will be fair weather; for the sky is red. And in the morning, it will be foul weather today: for the sky is red and lowring.

—Matthew 16.2—3

The fog comes
on little cat feet.
It sits looking
over the harbor and city
on silent haunches
and then, moves on.

—Carl Sandburg

COMMUNITY

Now the vicissitudes that afflict the individual have their source in society. ... Personal relations have given way to impersonal ones. The Great Society has arrived and the task of our generation is to bring it under control.

—Aneurin Bevan

[Society] is a partnership in all science, a partnership in all art, a partnership in every virtue and in all perfection. As the ends of such a partnership cannot be obtained in many generations, it becomes a partnership not only between those who are living, but between those who are living, those who are dead, and those who are to be born.

—Edmund Burke

We must be beware of trying to build a society in which nobody counts for anything except a politician or an official, a society where enterprise gains no reward and thrift no privileges.

—Winston Churchill

The principles of Jefferson are the definitions and axioms of free society.

—Abraham Lincoln

CONFIDENCE

Nobody can make you feel inferior without your consent.

—Eleanor Roosevelt

It took me a long time not to judge myself through someone else's eyes.

—Sally Field

Don't let people drive you crazy when you know it's in walking distance.

—Author Unknown

Our remedies oft in ourselves do lie
Which we ascribe to heaven.

—William Shakespeare, *All's Well That Ends Well*

A successful person is one who can lay a firm foundation with the bricks that others throw at him or her.

—David Brinkley

It's not who you are that holds you back, it's who you think you're not.

—Author Unknown

We have to learn to be our own best friends because we fall too easily into the trap of being our own worst enemies.

—Roderick Thorp, *Rainbow Drive*

It ain't what they call you, it's what you answer to.

—W.C. Fields

Whether you think you can or think you can't — you are right.

—Henry Ford

I quit being afraid when my first venture failed and the sky didn't fall down.

—Allen H. Neuharth

If you hear a voice within, you say "you cannot paint," then by all means paint, and that voice will be silenced.

—Vincent Van Gogh

Make the most of yourself, for that is all there is of you.

—Ralph Waldo Emerson

I am convinced all of humanity is born with more gifts than we know. Most are born geniuses and just get de—geniused rapidly.

—Buckminster Fuller

People are like stained—glass windows. They sparkle and shine when the sun is out, but when the darkness sets in their true beauty is revealed only if there is light from within.

—Elisabeth Kübler—Ross

Don't live down to expectations. Go out there and do something remarkable.

—Wendy Wasserstein

Success comes in cans, not cant's.

—Author Unknown

Put your future in good hands — your own.

—Author Unknown

I am not a has—been. I am a will be.

—Lauren Bacall

I'm not old enough to play baseball or football. I'm not eight yet. My mom told me when you start baseball, you aren't going to be able to run that fast because you had an operation. I told mom I wouldn't need to run that fast. When I play baseball, I'll just hit them out of the park. Then I'll be able to walk.

—Edward J. McGrath, Jr.

If you really put a small value upon yourself, rest assured that the world will not raise your price.

—Author Unknown

Confidence comes not from always being right but from not fearing to be wrong.

—Peter T. Mcintyre

Life shrinks or expands in proportion to one's courage.

—Anaïs Nin, *Diary*, 1969

Argue for your limitations and, sure enough, they're yours.

—Richard Bach, *Illusions*

You have to expect things of yourself before you can do them.

—Michael Jordan

It is not the mountain we conquer but ourselves.

—Edmund Hillary

Thousands of geniuses live and die undiscovered — either by themselves or by others.

—Mark Twain

Nothing splendid has ever been achieved except by those who dared believe that something inside of them was superior to circumstance.

—Bruce Barton

A great deal of talent is lost to the world for want of a little courage. Every day sends to their graves obscure men whose timidity prevented them from making a first effort.

—Sydney Smith

Pay no attention to what the critics say. A statue has never been erected in honor of a critic.

—Jean Sibelius

Aerodynamically the bumblebee shouldn't be able to fly, but the bumblebee doesn't know that so it goes on flying anyway.

—Mary Kay Ash

The courage to be is the courage to accept oneself, in spite of being unacceptable.

—Paul Tillich

Of all our infirmities, the most savage is to despise our being.

—Michel de Montaigne

People are crying up the rich and variegated plumage of the peacock, and he is himself blushing at the sight of his ugly feet.

—Sa'Di

It's hard to fight an enemy who has outposts in your head.

—Sally Kempton, *Esquire*, 1970

When the grass looks greener on the other side of the fence, it may be that they take better care of it there.

—Cecil Selig

Other people's opinion of you does not have to become your reality.

—Les Brown

You have brains in your head.
You have feet in your shoes.
You can steer yourself in any direction you choose.
You're on your own.
And you know what you know.
You are the guy who'll decide where to go.

—Dr. Seuss

Confidence is preparation. Everything else is beyond your control.

—Richard Kline

Appeal is fifty percent what you've got and fifty percent what people think you've got.

—Sophia Loren

Knock the "t" off the "can't."

—Samuel Johnson

All of us have wonders hidden in our breasts, only needing circumstances to evoke them.

—Charles Dickens

They are the weakest, however strong, who have no faith in themselves or their own powers.

—Christian Bovee

If you doubt yourself, then indeed you stand on shaky ground.

—Henrik Ibsen

We are all such a waste of our potential, like three-way lamps using one-way bulbs.

—Mignon McLaughlin, *The Neurotic's Notebook*, 1960

What lies behind us and what lies before us are tiny matters compared to what lies within us.

—Ralph Waldo Emerson

If we all did the things we are capable of doing, we would literally astound ourselves.

—Thomas Alva Edison

Always hold your head up, but be careful to keep your nose at a friendly level.

—Max L. Forman

Our doubts are traitors, and make us lose the good we oft might win, by fearing to attempt.

—William Shakespeare, *Measure for Measure*, 1604

The things we hate about ourselves aren't more real than things we like about ourselves.

—Ellen Goodman

I was thinking of my patients, and how the worst moment for them was when they discovered they were masters of their own fate. It was not a matter of bad or good luck. When they could no longer blame fate, they were in despair.

—Anaïs Nin

Just as much as we see in others we have in ourselves.

—William Hazlitt

Your problem is you're … too busy holding onto your unworthiness.

—Ram Dass

Learning too soon our limitations, we never learn our powers.

—Mignon McLaughlin, *The Neurotic's Notebook*, 1960

Lend yourself to others, but give yourself to yourself.

—Michel de Montaigne

It's me who is my enemy
Me who beats me up
Me who makes the monsters
Me who strips my confidence.

—Paula Cole, "Me," *This Fire*

The man who acquires the ability to take full possession of his own mind, may take possession of anything else to which he is justly entitled.

—Andrew Carnegie

Life marks us all down, so it's just as well that we start out by overpricing ourselves.

—Mignon McLaughlin, *The Neurotic's Notebook*, 1960

A gold medal is a nice thing — but if you're not enough without it, you'll never be enough with it.

—From *Cool Runnings*

If I am not for myself, who will be?

—Pirke Avoth

Self-love seems so often unrequited.

—Anthony Powell

Once you become self-conscious, there is no end to it; once you start to doubt, there is no room for anything else.

—Mignon McLaughlin, *The Neurotic's Notebook*, 1960

What a man thinks of himself, that it is which determines, or rather indicates his fate.

—Henry David Thoreau

There are offences given and offences not given but taken.

—Izaak Walton

A person can grow only as much as his horizon allows.

—John Powell

Plant your own garden and decorate your own soul, instead of waiting for someone to bring you flowers.

—Veronica A. Shoffstall, *"After a While," 1971*

It is folly for a man to pray to the gods, for that which he has the power to obtain by himself.

—Epicurus

If you must love your neighbor as yourself, it is at least as fair to love yourself as your neighbor.

—Nicholas de Chamfort

I am not afraid of storms, for I am learning how to sail my ship.

—Louisa May Alcott

Every day we slaughter our finest impulses. That is why we get a heart-ache when we read those lines written by the hand of a master and recognize them as our own, as the tender shoots which we stifled because we lacked the faith to believe in our own powers, our own criterion of truth and beauty. Every man, when he gets quiet, when he becomes desperately honest with himself, is capable of uttering profound truths. We all derive from the same source. There is no mystery about the origin of things. We are all part of creation, all kings, all poets, all musicians; we have only to open up, to discover what is already there.

—Henry Miller, *Sexus*

Self-confidence grows on trees, in other people's orchards.

—Mignon McLaughlin, *The Neurotic's Notebook*, 1960

When there is no enemy within, the enemies outside cannot hurt you.

—African Proverb

The best way to gain self-confidence is to do what you are afraid to do.

—Author Unknown

Be humble, for the worst thing in the world is of the same stuff as you; be confident, for the stars are of the same stuff as you.

—Nicholai Velimirovic

Shyness has a strange element of narcissism, a belief that how we look, how we perform, is truly important to other people.

—André Dubus

Chiefly the mold of a man's fortune is in his own hands.

—Francis Bacon

God wisely designed the human body so that we can neither pat our own backs nor kick ourselves too easily.

—Author Unknown

We probably wouldn't worry about what people think of us if we could know how seldom they do.

—Olin Miller

You're never as good as everyone tells you when you win, and you're never as bad as they say when you lose.

—Lou Holtz and John Heisler, *The Fighting Spirit*

Self assurance is contemptible and fatal unless it is self-knowledge.

—George Santayana, *Character and Opinion in the United States*, 1921

Mediocrity is a hand-rail.

—Charles Louis de Secondat, Baron de Montesquieu, *Mes pensées*

There is no need to reach high for the stars. They are already within you — just reach deep into yourself!

—Tas Soft Wind

All that Adam had, all that Caesar could, you have and can do.... Build, therefore, your own world.

—Ralph Waldo Emerson, *Nature*

Oliver Wendell Holmes once attended a meeting in which he was the shortest man present. "Dr. Holmes," quipped a friend, "I should think you'd feel rather small among us big fellows." "I do," retorted Holmes, "I feel like a dime among a lot of pennies."

—Author Unknown

The way you treat yourself sets the standard for others.

—Sonya Friedman

Our ordinary mind always tries to persuade us that we are nothing but acorns and that our greatest happiness will be to become bigger, fatter, shinier acorns; but that is of interest only to pigs. Our faith gives us knowledge of something better: that we can become oak trees.

—E.F. Schumacher

Many men are like unto sausages: whatever you stuff them with, that they will bear in them.

—Alexi Konstantinovich Tolstoy

Only as high as I reach can I grow,
Only as far as I seek can I go,
Only as deep as I look can I see,
Only as much as I dream can I be.

—Karen Ravn

Our deepest fear is not that we are inadequate. Our deepest fear is that we are powerful beyond measure. It is our light, not our darkness, that most frightens us. We ask ourselves, who am I to be brilliant, gorgeous, talented, fabulous? Actually, who are you not to be? You are a child of God. Your playing small doesn't serve the world. There's nothing enlightened about shrinking so that other people won't feel insecure around you. We are all meant to shine, as children do. We were born to make manifest the glory of God that is within us. It's not just in some of us; it's in everyone. And as we let our own light shine, we unconsciously give other people permission to do the same. As we're liberated from our own fear, our presence automatically liberates others.

—Marianne Williamson, *A Return to Love: Reflections on the Principles of a Course in Miracles*, 1992

Men are not against you; they are merely for themselves.

—Gene Fowler, *Skyline*, 1961

CURSE

Let fever sweat them till they tremble
Cramp rack their limbs till they resemble
Cartoons by Goya:
Their daughters sterile be in rut,
May cancer rot their herring gut,
The circular madness on them shut, Or paranoia

—W. H. Auden, *On This Island*

He cursed him at board, he cursed him in bed;
From the sole of his foot to the crown of his head;
He cursed him in sleeping, that every night
He should dream of the devil, and wake in a fright;
He cursed him in eating, he cursed him in drinking,
He cursed him in coughing, in sneezing, in winking;
He cursed him in sitting, in standing, in lying;
He cursed him in walking, in riding, in flying;
He cursed him in living, he cursed him in dying!

—R. H. Barham, *The Jackdaw of Rheims*

I shall curse you with book and bell and candle.

—Sir Thomas Malory, *Morte d'Arthur*

Weary se'n—nights nine times nine
Shall he dwindle, peak and pine.'

—Shakespeare, *Macbeth, 1, 3*

All the infections that the sun sucks up
From bogs, fens, flats, on Prosper fall, and make him
By inch—meal a disease.

—Shakespeare, *The Tempest. 11, 2*

May the strong curse of crossed affections light

Back on thy bosom with reflected blight!
And make thee in thy leprosy of mind
As loathsome to thyself as to mankind!

—Shelley, To the *Lord Chancellor* (Weldon)

Cursed be the social wants that sin against the strength of youth!
Cursed be the social lies that warp us from the living truth!
Cursed be the sickly forms that err from honest Nature's rule!
Cursed be the gold that gilds the straiten'd forehead of the fool!

—Tennyson, *Locksley Hall*

DEATH

Marley was dead: to begin with ... Old Marley was as dead as a door nail

—Dickens, *A Christmas Carol*

Let the dead bury their dead.

—New Testament, *Matthew, VIII, 22*

When I am dead, my dearest,
Sing no sad songs for me;
Plant thou no roses at my head,
Nor shady cypress tree:
Be the green grass above me
With showers and dewdrops wet;
And if thou wilt, remember,
And if thou wilt, forget.

—Christina Rossetti, *Song*

Strew on her roses, roses,
And never a spray of yew.
In quiet she reposes:
Ah I would that I did too.

—Matthew Arnold, *Requiescat*

O Death! the poor man's dearest friend
The kindest and the best.

—Burns, Man Was *Made* to Mourn

Da spreeng ees con; but oh, da joy
Eet is too late!
He was so cold. my leetia boy, He no could wait.

—T. A. Daly, Do *Leetta Boy*

Afraid? Of whom am I afraid?
Not Death, for who is He?
The porter of my father's lodge as much abasheth me.

—Emily Dickinson, *Time and Eternity*

Death be not proud, though some have called thee
Mighty and dreadful, for thou art not so,
For, those, whom thou think'st, thou dost overthrow,
Die not, poor death, nor yet canst thou kill me ...
death, thou shalt die.

—John Donne, *Holy Sonnet; X*

Account ye no man happy till he die.

—Euripides, *Daughters of Troy*

The little toy dog is covered with dust,
But sturdy and staunch he stands;
And the little toy soldier is red with rust,
And his musket moulds in his hands;
Time was when the little toy dog was new,
And the soldier was passing fair;
And that was the time when our Little Boy Blue
Kissed them and put them there.

—Eugene Field, *Little Boy Blue*

Can storied urn or animated bust
Back to its mansion call the fleeting breath?
Can Honour's voice provoke the silent dust,
Or Flattery soothe the dull cold ear of Death?

—Gray, *Elegy Written in a Country Churchyard*

When life is woe,
And hope is dumb,
The World says, "Go!"
The Grave says, "Come!"

—Arthur Guiterman, *Betel—Nuts*

One more unfortunate,
Weary of breath,
Rashly importunate
Gone to her death!
Take her up tenderly,
Lift her with care;
Fashioned so slenderly,
Young, and so fair!

—Thomas Hood, *The Bridge of Sighs*

Our very hopes belied our fears,
Our fears our hopes belied;
We thought her dying when she slept,
And sleeping when she died.

—Thomas Hood. *The Death—Bed*

Pale death, with impartial step, knocks at the poor man's cottage and the palaces of kings.
(Pallida Mors aequo pulsat pede …)

—Horace, *Odes, l, 4*

With rue my heart is laden

For golden friends I had,
For many a rose—lipt maiden
And many a lightfoot lad.

—A. E. Housman, A *Shropshire Lad*

Ah, what avails the sceptred race,
Ah, what the form divine!
What every virtue, every grace!
Rose Aylmer all were thine.
Rose Aylmner whom these wakeful eyes
May weep, but never see,
A night of memories and sighs
I consecrate to thee.

—W. S. Landor, Rose *Aylmer*

There is a reaper, whose name is Death,
And with his sickle keen,
He reaps the bearded grain at a breath,
And the flowers that grow between.

—Longfellow, *The Reaper and the Flowers*

I am dying, Egypt, dying,
Ebbs the crimson life-tide fast,
And the dark Plutonian shadows
Gather on the evening blast.

—W.H. Lytle, *Antony and Cleopatra* (the first line is from Shakespeare)

Around, around the sun we go:
The moon goes round the earth.
We do not die of death:
We die of vertigo.

—Archibald Macleish, *Mother Goose's Garland*

But O the heavy change, now thou art gone,
Now thou art gone and never must return!

—Milton, *Lycidas*

So we must part, my body, you and I
Who've spent so many pleasant years together.
Tis sorry work to lose your company
Who clove to me so close,

—Cosmo Monkhouse, *Any Soul to Any Body*

And grant me, when I face the grisly Thing,
One haughty cry to pierce the gray Perhaps!
O let me be a tune-swept fiddlestring
That feels the Master Melody—and *snaps.*

—J. G. Neihardt, *Let Me Give Out My Years*

O eloquent, just, and mighty Death! whom none could advise, thou hast persuaded; what none hath dared, thou hast done; ... thou hast drawn together all the far—stretched greatness, all the pride, cruelty, and ambition of man, and covered it over with these two narrow words, *Hic jacet!*

—Sir Walter Raleigh. *History* of *the World, V*

Out of the chill and the shadow,
Into the thrill and the shrine;
Out of the death and the famine,
Into the fulness divine.

—Mabgarlte. Sangster, *Going Home*

Like the dew on the mountain,
Like the foam on the river,
Like the bubble on the fountain,
Thou art gone, and for ever!

—Walter Scott, *The Lady* of *the Lake*

I have a rendezvous with Death
At some disputed barricade....
And I to my pledged word am true,
I shall not fail that rendezvous.

—Alan Seeger, I *Have a Rendezvous with Death*

.... death,
The undiscovered country, from whose bourn
No traveller returns.

—Shakespeare, *Hamlet, III, 1*

Fear no more the heat o' the sun
Nor the furious winters rages;
Thou thy worldly task hast done,
Home art gone and ta'en thy wages.

—Shakespeare, *Cymbeline, IV, 2*

Golden lads and girls all must,
As chimney-sweepers, come to dust.

—Shakespeare, *Cymbeline, IV, 2*

After life's fitful fever, he sleeps well;
Treason has done his worst: nor steel nor poison,
Malice domestic, foreign levy, nothing
Can touch him further.

—Shakespeare, *Macbeth, 111, 2*

The weariest and most loathed worldly life
That age, ache, penury, and imprisonment
Can lay on nature, is a paradise
To what we fear of death.

—Shakespeare, *Measure for Measure, III. 1*

Come away, come away, death.
And in sad cypress let me be laid;

Fly away, fly away, breath:
I am slain by a fair cruel maid.
My shroud of white, stuck all with yew,
O, prepare its my part of death, no one so true
Did share it.

—Shakespeare, *Twelfth Night, 11, 4*

Death is here and death is there,
Death is busy everywhere,
All around, within, beneath,
Above is death—and we are death.

—Shelley, *Death (1820)*

Sunset and evening star,
And one clear call for mel
And may there be no moaning of the bar
When I put out to sea.

… … … … … … … … … .

I hope to see my Pilot face to face
When I have crost the bar.

—Tennyson, *Crossing the Bar*

She lived unknown, and few could know
When Lucy ceased to be;
But she is in her grave, and, oh,
The difference to me!

—Wordsworth, *She Dwelt Among the Untrodden Ways*

Death is a black camel, which kneels at the gates of all.

—Abd-el-Kader

It is good to die before one has done anything deserving death.

—Ananandrides

Men fear death as children fear to go in the dark; and as that natural fear in children is increased with tales, so is the other.

—Francis Bacon

It is as natural to man to die, as to be born; and to a little infant, perhaps the one is as painful as the other.

—Francis Bacon

He that unburied lies wants not his hearse,
For unto him a Tomb's the Universe.

—Thomas Browne

We all labor against our own cure, for death is the cure of all diseases.

—Thomas Browne

The fear of death is worse than death.

—Robert Burton

Ah, surely nothing dies but something mourns!

—Lord Byron

Death levels all things.

—Claudian

Death is the liberator of him whom freedom cannot release; the physician of him whom medicine cannot cure; the comforter of him whom time cannot console.

—Charles Caleb Colton

O death, where is thy sting?
O grave, where is thy victory?

—I Corinthians 15:55

These have not the hope of death.

—Dante

Dead men tell no tales.

—English Proverb

There were some who said that a man at the point of death was more free than all others, because death breaks every bond, and over the dead the united world has no power.

—Fènelon

Dust thou art, and unto dust shalt thou return.

—Genesis 3:19

Show me the manner in which a nation or a community cares for its dead. I will measure exactly the sympathies of its people, their respect for the laws of the land, and their loyalty to high ideals.

—Attributed to William E. Gladstone

Death is Nature's expert advice to get plenty of life.

—Goethe

We die ourselves a little every time we kill in others something that deserved to live.

—Oscar Hammling

How frighteningly few are the persons whose death would spoil our appetite and make the world seem empty.

—Eric Hoffer

It is not right to glory in the slain.

—Homer

'Tis after death that we measure men.

—James Barron Hope

Sweet and glorious it is to die for our country.

—Horace

In the democracy of the dead all men at last are equal. There is neither rank nor station nor prerogative in the republic of the grave.

—John James Ingalls

Depend upon it, Sir, when a man knows he is to be hanged in a fortnight, it concentrates his mind wonderfully.

—Samuel Johnson

I have been half in love with easeful death,
Call'd him soft names in many a mused rhyme.

—John Keats

So now he is a legend when he would have preferred to be a man.

—Jacqueline Kennedy

Were a star quenched on high,
For ages would its light,
Still travelling downward from the sky,
Shine on our mortal sight.
So when a great man dies,
For years beyond our ken,
The light he leaves behind him lies
Upon the paths of men.

—Henry Wadsworth Longfellow

There is no death! What seems so is transition; this life of mortal breath is but a suburb of the life elysian, whose portal we call death.

—Henry Wadsworth Longfellow

A man's dying is more the survivors' affair than his own.

—Thomas Mann

The grave's a fine and private place,
But none, I think, do there embrace.

—Andrew Marvell

Death has a thousand doors to let out life.
I shall find one.

—Philip Messinger

Whom the gods love dies young.

—Menander

Death is the golden key of eternity.

—John Milton

Death seems to provide the minds of the Anglo-Saxon race with a greater fund of innocent amusement than any other single subject.

—Dorothy L. Sayers

Death is a punishment to some, to some a gift, and to many a favor.

—Seneca

Nothing in his life became him like the leaving it.

—Shakespeare

Imperious Caesar, dead and turn'd to clay, Might stop a hole to keep the wind away.

—Shakespeare

To die—to sleep,
No more, and by that sleep to say we end
The heart—ache and the thousand natural shocks
That flesh is heir to....

—Shakespeare

Say nothing but good of the dead.

—Solon

Do not go gentle into that good night,
Old age should burn and rave at close of day;
Rage, rage against the dying of the light.

—Dylan Thomas

DEMOCRACY

The Republic needed to be passed through chastening, purifying fires of adversity and suffering: so these came and did their work and the verdure of a new national life springs greenly, luxuriantly, from their ashes.

—Horace Greeley

But every difference of opinion is not a difference of principle. We have called by different names brethren of the same principle. We are all republicans—we are federalists.

—Thomas Jefferson

EDUCATION

Nothing in education is so astonishing as the amount of ignorance it accumulates in the form of inert facts.

—Henry Adams, *The Education of Henry Adams*

What's a' your jargon o' your schools,
Your Latin names for horns and stools;
If honest Nature made you fools.

—Burns, *First Epistle to J. Lapraik*

Better build schoolrooms for "the boy,"
Than cells and gibbets for "the Man."

—Eliza Cook, A Song for *the Ragged Schools*

When you don't have an education, you've got to use your brains.

—Anonymous

The educated differ from the uneducated as much as the living from the dead.

—Attributed to Aristotle

The aim of education should be to teach us rather how to think, than what to think ...

—James Beattie

Education is the cheap defence of nations.

—Attributed to Edmund Burke

Upon the education of the people of this country the fate of this country depends.

—Benjamin Disraeli

An education isn't how much you have committed to memory, or even how much you know. It's being able to differentiate between what you do know and what you don't. It's knowing where to go to find out what you need to know; and it's knowing how to use the information you get.

—Attributed to William Feather

Enlighten the people generally, and tyranny and oppressions of body and mind will vanish like evil spirits at the dawn of day.

—Thomas Jefferson

If you plan for a year, plant a seed. If for ten years, plant a tree. If for a hundred years, teach the people. When you sow a seed once, you will reap a single harvest. When you teach the people, you will reap a hundred harvests.

—Kuan Chung

Learned Institutions ought to be favorite objects with every free people. They throw that light over the public mind which is the best security against crafty & dangerous encroachments on the public liberty.

—James Madison

What spectacle can be more edifying or more seasonable, than that of Liberty & Learning, each leaning on the other for their mutual & surest support?

—James Madison

Education, then, beyond all other devices of human origin, is the great equalizer of the conditions of men,—the balance—wheel of the social machinery.

—Horace Mann

I have never let my schooling interfere with my education.

—Mark Twain

ERA

To every thing there is a season,
and time to every purpose under the heaven:
A time to be born, and a time to die;
a time to plant, and a time to pluck up
that which is planted;
A time to kill, and a time to heal;
a time to break down, and a time to build up;
A time to weep, and a time to laugh;
a time to mourn, and a time to dance;
A time to cast away stones, and a time to
gather stones together;
a time to embrace, and a time to refrain
from embracing;
A time to get, and a time to lose;
a time to keep, and a time to cast away;
A time to rend, and a time to sew;
a time to keep silence, and a time to speak;

A time to love, and a time to hate;
a time of war, and a time of peace.
—Ecclesiastes 3:1—8

"The time has come," the Walrus said,
"To talk of many things:
Of shoes—and ships—and sealing wax—
Of cabbages—and kings—
And why the sea is boiling hot—
And whether pigs have wings."
—Lewis Carroll

There is no time like the old time,
when you and I were young,
When the buds of April blossomed,
and the birds of spring-time sung!
The garden's brightest glories
by summer suns are nursed,
But oh, the sweet, sweet violets,
the flowers that opened first!
—Oliver Wendell Holmes

Time is at once the most valuable and the most perishable of all our possessions.

—John Randolph of Roanoke

It was the best of times, it was the worst of times, it was the age of wisdom, it was the age of foolishness, it was the epoch of belief, it was the epoch of incredulity, it was the season of Light, it was the season of Darkness, it was the spring of hope, it was the winter of despair, we had everything before us, we had nothing before us, we were all going direct to Heaven, we were all going direct the other way—in, short, the period was so far like the present period, that some of its noisiest authorities insisted on its being received, for good or for evil, in the superlative degree of comparison only.

—Charles Dickens

These times of ours are serious and full of calamity, but all times are essentially alike. As soon as there is life there is danger.

—Ralph Waldo

This time, like all times, is a very good one, if we but know what to do with it.

—Ralph Waldo Emerson

These are the times that try men's souls. The summer soldier and the sunshine patriot will, in this crisis, shrink from the service of their country; but he that stands it now, deserves the love and thanks of man and woman.

—Thomas Paine

On the Plains of Hesitation bleach the bones countless millions who, at the Dawn of Victory, ; down to wait, and waiting—died!

—George W. Cecil

A clear strong statement of a case if made too soon or too late fails. If well made at the right time it is effective. It is a nice point to study the right time.

—James A. Garfield

EXPENDITURE

Nothing is easier than spending the public money. It does not appear to belong to anybody. The temptation is overwhelming to bestow it on somebody.

—Attributed to Calvin Coolidge

A billion here, a billion there, and pretty soon you're talking about real money.

—Attributed to Senator Everett M. Dirksen

That most delicious of all privileges—spending other people's money.

—John Randolph of Roanoke

Lord, the money we do spend on Government and it's not one bit better than the government we got for onethird the money twenty years ago.

—Will Rogers

EXPRESSIONS (words)

"When *I* use a word," Humpty Dumpty said, in rather a scornful tone, "it means just what I choose it to mean—neither more nor less." 'The question is," said Alice, "whether you can make words mean so many different things." "The question is" said Humpty Dumpty, "which is to be master—that's all."

—Lewis Carrol

A word is not a crystal, transparent and unchanged, it is the skin of a living thought and may vary greatly in color and content according to the circumstances and the time in which it is used.

—Oliver Wendell Holmes

In Words, as Fashions, the same Rule will hold;
Alike Fantastick, if too *New*, or Old;
Be not the first by whom the *New* are try'd,
Nor yet the last to lay the Old aside.

—Alexander Pope

EXPRESSION(speaking out)

Discretion in speech, is more than eloquence.

—Francis Bacon

... Why, if any of you young gentlemen have a mind to get heard a mile off, you must make a bonfire of your reputation, and a close enemy of most men who wish you well. And what will you get in return? Well, if I must for the benefit of the economists, charge you up with some selfish gain, I will say that you get the satisfaction of having been heard, and that this is the whole possible scope of human ambition.

—John Jay Chapman

Least said, soonest mended.

—Charles Dickens

Without Freedom of Thought, there can be no such Thing as Wisdom; and no such Thing as publick Liberty, without Freedom of Speech.

—Benjamin Franklin

Every absurdity has a champion to defend it, for error is always talkative.

—Oliver Goldsmith

Every time we turn our heads the other way when we see the law flouted—when we tolerate what we know to be wrong—when we close our eyes and ears to the corrupt because we are too busy, or too frightened—when we fail to speak up and speak out—we strike a blow against freedom and decency and justice.

—Robert F. Kennedy

Nature has given us two ears, two eyes, and but one tongue, to the end that we should hear and see more than we speak.

—Socrates

FAILURE

They never fail who die
In a great cause: the block may soak their gore;
Their heads may sodden in the sun; their limbs
Be strung to city gates and castle walls—
But still their spirit walks abroad.

—Byron, *Marino Faliero, II, 2*

And nothing to look backward to with pride,
And nothing to look forward to with hope.

—Robert Frost, *The Death of the Hired Man*

They went forth to battle, but they always fell.

—James Macpherson (Ossian), *Cath—loda*

I sing the hymn of the conquered, who fall in the battle of life,
The hvmn of the wounded, the beaten who died over whelmed in the strife.

—W. W. Story, *lo Victis*

We are all of us failures—at least, the best of us are.

—James Matthew Barrie

A man's life is interesting primarily when he has failed—I well know. For it's a sign that he tried to surpass himself.

—Georges Clemenceau

I never blame failure—there are too many complicated situations in life—but I am absolutely merciless towards lack of effort.

—F. Scott Fitzgerald

One who fears failure limits his activities. Failure is only the opportunity to more intelligently begin again.

—Henry Ford

Not failure, but low aim, is crime.

—James Russell Lowell

I have no use for men who fail. The cause of their failure is no business of mine, but I want successful men as my associates.

—John D. Rockefeller

It is hard to fail, but it is worse never to have tried to succeed.

—Theodore Roosevelt

Ambition is the last refuge of the failure.

—Unknown

FAITH

Trust men and they will be true to you; treat them greatly and they will show themselves great.

—Ralph Waldo Emerson

Preserve me, O God: for in thee do I put my trust.

—Psalms 16:1.

We have a saying in the movement that we don't trust anybody over 30.

—Jack Weinberg

FIGURES

The individual source of the statistics may easily be the weakest link.

—Josiah stamp

There are three kinds of lies: lies, damned lies, and statistics.

—Mark Twain

GENIUS

Doing easily what others find difficult is talent: doing what is impossible *for talent is* genius.

—Amiel, *Journal.* Dec. 17, 1856

The eagle never lost so much time as when he submitted to learn of the crow.

—Blake, *Proverbs of Hell*

Great wits are sure to madness near allied,
And thin partitions do their bounds divide.

—Dryden, *Absalom and Achitophel, I*

Genius is one per cent inspiration and ninety-nine per cent perspiration.

—Thomas A. Edison, *Newspaper Interview, 1931*

Gift, like genius, I often think means only an infinite capacity for taking pains.

—Jane E. Hopkins, *Work Amongst Working Men*

Talk not of genius baffled. Genius is master of man.
Genius does what it must, and Talent does what it can.

—Owen Meredith, *Last Words of a Sensitive Second—rate Poet*

Genius, cried the commuter,
As he ran for the 8:13,
Consists of an infinite capacity
For catching trains.

—Christopher Morley, *The Commuter*

When a true genius appears in the world, you may know him by this sign, that the dunces are all in a confederacy against him.

—Swift, *Thoughts* on *Various Subjects*

I have nothing to declare except my genius.

—Oscar Wilde, To revenue officers in America, 1882

Doing easily what others find difficult is talent; doing what is impossible for talent is genius.

—Henri-Frederic Amiel

I have known no man of genius who had not to pay, in some affliction or defect either physical or spiritual, for what the gods had given him.

—Max Beerbohm

Talent, lying in the understanding, is often inherited; genius, being the action of reason and imagination, rarely or never.

—Samuel Taylor Coleridge

Patience is a necessary ingredient of genius.

—Benjamin Disraeli

Genius must be born; it never can be taught.

—John Dryden

Every man of genius sees the world at a different angle from his fellows, and there is his tragedy.

—Havelock Ellis

Genius is the power of lighting one's own fire.

—John Foster

A man of genius makes no mistakes. His errors are volitional and are the portals of discovery.

—James Joyce

Genius is a promontory jutting out into the infinite.

—Victor Hugo

Genius begets great works; labor alone finished them.

—Joseph Joubert

One science only will one genius fit;
So vast is art, so narrow human wit.

—Alexander Pope

The poets' scrolls will outlive the monuments of stone. Genius survives; all else is claimed by death.

—Edmund Spenser

There is a certain characteristic common to all those whom we call geniuses. Each of them has a consciousness of being a man apart.

—Miguel de Unamuno

HAPPINESS

That action is best which procures the greatest happiness for the greatest numbers.

—Francis Hutcheson. An *Inquiry* into ... *Beauty* and Virtue

Happiness is the only good, reason the only torch, justice the only worship, humanity the only religion, and love the only priest.

—R. G. Ingersoll, A Tribute to Eben Ingersoll

Glad that I live am I;
That the sky is blue;
Glad for the country lanes,
And the fall of dew.

—Lizette W. Reese, A Little Song *of Life*

O, how bitter a thing it is to look into happiness through another man's eyes!

—Shakespeare, As You *Like* It. V, 2

You have no more right to consume happiness without producing it than to consume wealth without producing it.

—Bernard Shaw, *Candida.* I

Ye seek for happiness—alas, the dayl
Ye find it not in luxury nor in gold,
Nor in the fame, nor in the envied sway
For which, O willing slaves to Custom old,
Severe taskmistress! ye your hearts have sold.

—Shelley, *The Revolt Of Islam.* XI

Oh. make us happy and you make us good.

—R. Browning, The Ring and the Book, IV

Now the heart is so full that a drop overfills it,
We are happy now because God wills it.

—J. R. Lowell, *The* Vision of Sir *Launfal,* Prelude

Let not thy left hand know what thy right hand doeth.

—*New Testament: Matthew, V1, 3*

Many hands make light work.

—Proverb

All the perfumes of Arabia will not sweeten this little hand.

—Shakespeare

Hold him alone truly fortunate who has ended his life in happy well-being.

—Aeschylus

Happiness is at once the best, the noblest and the pleasantest of things.

—Aristotle

Happiness sneaks in through a door you didn't know you left open.
—John Barrymore

What is given by the gods more desirable than a happy hour?
—Catullus

The happiness of life is made up of minute fractions—the little soon forgotten charities of a kiss or smile, a kind look, a heartfelt compliment, and the countless infinitesimals of pleasurable and genial feeling.
—Samuel Taylor Coleridge

To find out what one is fitted to do and to secure an opportunity to do it is the key to happiness.
—John Dewey

Happiness makes up in height for what it lacks in length.
—Robert Frost

Often the greatest enemy of present happiness is past happiness too well remembered.
—Oscar Hammling

And there is even a happiness
That makes the heart afraid.
—Thomas Hood

The supreme happiness of life is the conviction that we are loved.
—Victor Hugo

He is happiest of whom the world says least, good or bad.
—Thomas Jefferson

In order to be happy oneself it is necessary to make at least one other person happy ... The secret of human happiness is not in self—seeking but in self—forgetting.
—Theodore Reik

IDEAS

If a man take no thought about what is distant, he will find sorrow near at hand.

—Confucius

No brain is stronger than its weakest think.

—Thomas L. Masson

To him whose elastic and vigorous thought keeps pace with the sun, the day is a perpetual morning.

—Henry David Thoreau

IDENTITY

Nothing is easier than self-deceit. For what each man wishes, that he also believes to be true.

—Demosthenes

I now know all the people worth knowing in America, and I find no intellect comparable to my own.

—Margaret Fuller

The compulsion to take ourselves seriously is in inverse proportion to our creative capacity. When the creative flow dries up, all we have left is our importance.

—Eric Hoffer

... if at the end I have lost every other friend on earth I shall at least have one friend remaining and that one shall be down inside me.

—Attributed to Abraham Lincoln.

What we do belongs to what we are; and what we are is what becomes of us.

—Henry Van Dyke

IDEOLOGY

Teachers who educated children deserved more honour than parents who merely gave them birth; for bare life is furnished by the one, the other ensures a good life.

—Attributed to Aristotle

Give a man a fish and you feed him for a day. Teach a man to fish and you feed him for a lifetime.

—Chinese proverb

Who dares to teach must never cease to learn.

—John Cotton Dana

The whole art of teaching is only the art of awakening the natural curiosity of young minds for the purpose of satisfying it afterwards; and curiosity itself can be vivid and wholesome only in proportion as the mind is contented and happy.

—Anatole France

He who can, does. He who cannot, teaches.

—George Bernard Shaw

JEALOUSY

O, beware, my lord, of Jealousy:
It is the green—eyed monster which doth mock
The meat it feeds on.

—Shakespeare, *Othello, III, 3*

Trifles light as air
Are to the jealous confirmation strong
As proofs of holy writ.

—Shakespeare, *Othello, III*

I can endure my own despair,
But not another's hope.
—William Walsh, *Song*

Jealousy is … a tiger that tears not only its prey but also its own raging heart.
—Michael Beer

Anger and jealousy can no more bear to lose sight of their objects than love.
—George Eliot

Though jealousy be produced by love, as ashes are by fire, yet jealousy extinguishes love as ashes smother the flame.
—Margaret of Navarre

Love is strong as death; jealousy is cruel as the grave.
—Song of Solomon 8.6

JOY

There's not a joy the world can give like that it takes away,
—Byron. *Stanzas for Music*

All human joys are swift of wing,
For heaven doth so allot it,
That when you get an easy thing,
You find you haven't got it.
—Eugene Field, *Ways of Life*

Joy comes, grief goes; we know not how.
—J. R. Lowell, *The Vision of Sir Launfal*

Hence, vain deluding Joys,
The brood of Folly, without father bred.
—Milton, II *Penseroso*

At Earth's great market where Joy is trafficked in,
Buy while thy purse yet swells with golden Youth.

—Alan Seeger, *Ode to Antares*

I have drunken deep of joy,
And I will taste no other wine to-night.

—Shelley, *The Cenci, 1,3*

I found more joy in sorrow
Than you could find in joy.

—Sara Teasdale, *The Answer*

But we are pressed by heavy laws;
And often, glad no more,
We wear a face of joy, because
We have been glad of yore.

—Wordsworth, *The Fount*

Joy rises in me like a summer's morn.

—Samuel Taylor Coleridge

My theory is to enjoy life, but the practice is against it.

—Charles Lamb

My candle burns at both ends,
It will not last the night;
But ah, my foes, and oh, my friends,
It gives a lovely light!

—Edna St. Vincent Millay

Drink and dance and laugh and lie,
Love the reeling midnight through,
For tomorrow we shall die!
(But, alas, we never do.)

—Dorothy Parker

Weeping may endure for a night, but joy cometh in the morning.

—Psalms 30.5

A joy that's shared is a joy made double.

—John Ray

Occasionally in life there are those moments of unutterable fulfillment which cannot be completely Explained by those symbols called words. Their meanings can only be articulated by the inaudible language of the heart.

—Martin Luther King, Jr.

JUDGMENT

There, is so much good in the worst of us,
And so much bad in the best of us,
That, it hardly becomes any of us
To talk about the rest of us.

—Anon., Good *and Pad ;c. 1900)*

Judge not, that ye be not judged.

—New Testament, *Matthew,* VII, 1

Why beholdest thou the mote that is in thy brother's eye, but considerest not the beam that is in thy own eye?

—New Testament, *Matthew, VII, 3*

Thou art weighed in the balance, and art found wanting.

—Old Testament, *Daniel, V,* 27

Tis with our judgements as our watches, none
Go just alike, yet each believes his own.

—Pope, *Essay on Criticism, I*

O judgement! thou art fled to brutish beasts,
And men have lost their reason!

—Shakespeare, Julius *Caesar, III. 2*

Beware, so long as you live, of judging men by their outward appearance.

—Jean de La Fontaine

If we could first know where we are, and whither we are tending, we could then better judge what to do, and how to do it.

—Abraham Lincoln

We judge ourselves by what we feel capable of doing; others judge us by what we have done.

—Henry Wadsworth Longfellow

Everyone complains of the badness of his memory, but nobody of his judgment.

—Duc François de La Rochefoucauld

I mistrust the judgment of every man in a case in which his own wishes are concerned.

—Arthur Wellesley, Duke of Wellington

One cool judgment is worth a thousand hasty counsels. The thing to be supplied is light, not heat.

—Woodrow Wilson

KISS

The moth's kiss first!
Kiss me as if you made believe
You were not sure, this eve,
How my face, your flower, had pursed
is petals up.

—R. Browning, *In a Gondola*

Rose kissed me today.
Will she kiss me tomorrow?
Let it be as it may,
Rose kissed me today.

—Austin Dobson, A Kiss

The anatomical juxtaposition of two orbicularis oris muscles in a state of contraction.

—Dr. Henry Gibbons, *Definition of a Kiss*

Jenny kissed me when we met,
Jumping from the chair she sat in;
Time, you thief, who love to get
Sweets into your list, put that in!
Say I'm weary, say I'm sad,
Say that health and wealth have missed me:
Say I'm growing old, but add
Jenny kissed me,

—Leigh Hunt, *Jenny Kissed Me*

Leave a kiss but in the cup,
And I'll not look for wine.

—Ben Jonson, *To Celia*

Sweet Helen, make me immortal with a kiss!
Her lips suck forth my soul: see, where it flies!

—Christopher Marlowe, *Doctor Fautus*

A kiss, when all is said, what is it?
... a rosy dot
Placed on the "i" in loving; 'tis a secret
Told to the mouth instead of to the ear.

—Edmond Rostand, *Cyrano de Bergerac III*

Give me kisses Nay, 'tis true
I am just as rich as you;
And for every kiss I owe,
I can pay you back, you know,
Kiss me, then, Every moment—and again!

—J. G. Saxe, *To Lesbia* (after Catullus)

Dear as remembered kisses after death,
And sweet as those by hopeless fancy feign'd
On lips that are for others,

—Tennyson, The *Princess IV*

Gin a body meet a body
Comin' thro' the rye,
Gin a body kiss a body,
Need a body cry?

—Burns, *Comin, Thro' the Rye*

Oh, fie, Miss, you must not kiss and tell,

—Congreve, *Love for Love, II, 10*

A little time for laughter,
A little time to sing,
A little time to kiss and cling,
And no more kissing after.

—P. B, Marston, *After*

Yet whoop, Jackl Kiss Gillian the quicker,
Till she bloom like a rose, and a fig for the vicari

—Scott, *The Lady of the Lake, VI*

Take, O take those lips away,
That so sweetly were forsworn;

And those eyes, the break of day,
Lights that do mislead the morn:
But my kisses bring again, bring again;
Seals of love, but seal'd in vain, seal'd in vain.

—Shakespeare, *Measure for Measure, IV, 1*

See the mountains kiss high Heaven,
And the waves clasp one another;
No sister-flower would be forgiven
If it disdained its brother,
And the sunlight clasps the earth,
And the moonbeams kiss the sea:
What is all this sweet work worth,
If thou kiss not me?

—Shelley, *Love's Philosophy*

KNOWLEDGE

Knowledge is power.

—Hobbes, *Leviathan*

There are four sorts of men:
He who knows not and knows not he knows not: he is a fool—shun him; He who knows not and knows he knows not: he is simple —teach him. He who knows and knows not he knows: he is asleep—wake him; He who knows and knows he knows: he is wise—follow him.

—Lady Burton, In *Life of Sir Richard Burton* (quoted as an Arabian proverb)

Knowledge is the only instrument of production. that is not subject to diminishing returns,

—J. M. Clark, *Journal of Political Economy,* Oct., 1927

I have studied now Philosophy
And Jurisprudence, Medicine
And even, alas, Theology
From end to end with labor keen;
And here, poor fool, with all my lore
I stand no wiser than before,

—Goethe, *Faust, I (B,* Taylor trans.)

But knowledge to heir eyes her ample page,
Rich with the spoils of time, did ne'er unroll.

—Gray, *Elegy Written in a Country Churchyard*

All I know is what I read in the papers.

—Will Rogers

I know nothing except the tact of my ignorance.

—Socrates (quoted *in Diogenes Laertius*)

Knowledge comes, but wisdom lingers,

—Tennyson, *Locksley Hall*

To know that we know what we know, and that we do not know what we do not know, that is true knowledge,

—Thoreau. W *olden* (quoting Confucius)

What one knows is, in youth, of little moment; they know enough who know how to learn.

—Henry Adams

Knowledge is, indeed, that which, next to virtue, truly and essentially raises one man above another.

—Joseph Addison

A great deal of knowledge, which is not capable of making a man wise, has a natural tendency to make him vain and arrogant.

—Joseph Addison

The trouble with people is not that they dont know but that they know so much that ain't so.

— Attributed to Josh Billings (Henry Wheeler Shaw)

What little I do know I hope I am certain of.

—Josh Billings

I honestly believe it is better to know nothing than to know what ain't so.

—Josh Billings

Knowledge is a comfortable and necessary retreat and shelter for us in an advanced age; and if we do not plant it while young, it will give us no shade when we grow old.

—Lord Chesterfield

No technical knowledge can outweigh knowledge of the humanities, in the gaining of which philosophy and history walk hand in hand.

—Winston Churchill

The essence of knowledge is, having it, to apply it; not having it, to confess your ignorance.

—Confucius

The more extensive a man's knowledge of what has been done, the greater will be his power of knowing what to do.

—Benjamin Disraeli

If a man empties his purse into his head no one can take it away from him. An investment in knowledge always pays the best interest.

—Attributed to Benjamin Franklin

It is the province of knowledge to speak, and it is the privilege of wisdom to listen.

—Oliver Wendell Holmes

The benefits of education and of useful knowledge, generally diffused through a community, are essential to the preservation of a free government.

—Attributed to Sam Houston

Knowledge is of two kinds. We know a subject ourselves or we know where we can find information upon it.

—Samuel Johnson

Knowledge will forever govern ignorance: And a people who mean to be their own Governors, must arm themselves with the power which knowledge gives.

—James Madison

To myself I seem to have been only like a boy playing on the seashore, and diverting myself in now and then finding a smoother pebble, or a prettier shell than ordinary, whilst the great ocean of truth lay all undiscovered before me.

—Isaac Newton

Then I began to think, that it is very true which is commonly said, that the one—half of the world knoweth not how the other half liveth.

—Françols Rabelais

... They never open their mouths without subtracting from the sum of human knowledge.

—Thomas B. Reed

We have not the reverent feeling for the rainbow that a savage has, because we know how it is made. We have lost as much as we gained by prying into that matter.

—Mark Twain

Logic and metaphysics make use of more tools than all the rest of the sciences put together, and they do the least work.

—Charles Caleb Colton

Science without religion is lame, religion without science is blind.

—Albert Einstein

We give the name scientist to the type of man who has felt experiment to be a means guiding him to search out the deep truth of life, to lift a veil from its fascinating secrets, and who, in this pursuit, has felt arising within him a love for the mysteries of nature, so passionate as to annihilate the thought of himself.

—Maria Montessori

A new scientific truth does not triumph by convincing its opponents and making them see the light, but rather because its opponents eventually die, and a new generation grows up that is familiar with it.

—Max Planck

LABOUR

To labour is to pray,
(Laborare est orare.)

—Motto of the Benedictine monks

But the young, young children, O my brothers,
They are weeping bitterly!

They are weeping in the playtime of the others,
In the country of the free.

—E. B. Browning, *The Cry of the Children*

We labour soon, we labour late,
To feed the titled knave, man:
And a' the comfort we're to get
Is that ayont the grave, man,.

—Burns, *The Tree of Liberty*

If fifty men did all the work,
And gave the price to five,
And let those five make all the rules—
You'd say the fifty men were fools,
Unfit to be alive.

—Charlotte P. S, Gilman, *Five and Fifty*

Toil is the lot of all, and bitter woe
The fate of many,

—Homer, *Iliad, XXI* (Bryant trans.)

With fingers weary and worn,
With eyelids heavy and red,
A woman sat in unwomanly rags,
Plying her needle and thread.
....
O men with sisters dear,
O men with mothers and wives,
It is not linen you're wearing out,
But human creatures' lives!

—Thomas Hood, Song *of the Shirt*

I hold that if the Almighty had ever made a set of men that should do all the eating and none of the work. He would have made them with mouths only and no hands; and if He had ever made another class that He intent should do all the work and no eating. He would have made them with hands only and no mouths,

—Abraham Lincoln, *Mud-sill Theory of Labor*

Toiling—rejoicing—sorrowing,
Onward through life he goes;
Each morning sees some task begin,
Each evening sees it close;
Something attempted, something done,
Has earned a night's repose.

—Longfellow, *The Village Blacksmith*

Come unto me, all ye that labour and are heavy laden

—New Testament, *Matthew, XI, 28*

What profit hath a man of all his labour which he taketh under the sun?

—Old Testament, *Ecclesiastes, I,3*

Men of England, wherefore plough
For the lords who lay ye low?
Wherefore weave with toil and care
The rich robes your tyrants wear?

—Shelley, *Song*; To *the Men of England*

Labor conquers everything.
Labor *omnia* vincit.)

—Virgil, *Georgics, I*

There is no right to strike against the public safety by anybody, anywhere, anytime.

—Calvin Coolidge

Employment is nature's physician, and is essential to human happiness.

—Galen

Don't waste any time mourning—organize!

—Joe Hill

I've had the best possible chance of learning that what the working classes really need is to be allowed some part in the direction of public affairs, ...

—Henrik lbsen

Excellence in any department can be attained only by the labor of a lifetime; it is not to be purchased at a lesser price.

—Samuel Johnson

It ill behooves one who has supped at labor's table and who has been sheltered in labor's house to curse with equal fervor and fine impartiality both labor and its adversaries when they become locked in deadly embrace.

—John L. Lewis

Labor is prior to, and independent of, capital. Capital is only the fruit of labor, and could never have existed if labor had not first existed.

—Abraham Lincoln

The strongest bond of human sympathy, outside of the family relation, should be one uniting all working people, of all nations, and tongues, and kindreds.

—Abraham Lincoln

The labourer is worthy of his hire.

—Luke 10:7

Love, therefore, labor; if thou shouldst not want it for food, thou mayest for physic. It is wholesome to the body and good for the mind; it prevents the fruit of idleness.

—William Penn

No business which depends for existence on paying less than living wages to its workers has any right to continue …

—Franklin D. Roosevelt

I am a true labourer: I earn that I eat, get that I wear, owe no man hate, envy no man's happiness, glad of other men's good.

—Shakespeare

There is no real wealth but the labor of man. Were the mountains of gold and the valleys of silver, the world would not be one grain of corn the richer; not one comfort would be added to the human race.

—Percy B. Shelley

No race can prosper 'til it learns that there is as much dignity in tilling the field as in writing a poem.

—Booker T. Washington

Employment gives health, sobriety and morals. Constant employment and well—paid labor produce, in a country like ours, general prosperity, content, and cheerfulness.

—Daniel Webster

Nothing is really work unless you would rather be doing something else.

—Attributed to James M. Barrie

The most unhappy of all men is the man who cannot tell what he is going to do, who has got no work cut out for him in the world, and does not go into it.

—Thomas Carlyle

I think if I worked for a man I would work for him. I would not work for him a part of the time, and the rest of the time work against him. I would give an undivided service or none. If put to the pinch, an ounce of loyalty is worth a pound of cleverness.

—Elbert Hubbard

I long to accomplish a great and noble task, but it is my chief duty to accomplish humble tasks as though they were great and noble. The world is moved along, not only by the mighty shoves of its heroes, but also by the aggregate of the tiny pushes of each honest worker.

—Attributed to Helen Keller

You must obey this now for a Law, that he that will not worke shall not eate (except by sicknesse he be disabled:) for the labours, of thirtie or fortie honest and industrious men shall not be consumed to main—taine an hundred and fiftie idle loyterers.

—John smith

Drive a nail home and clinch it so faithfully that you can wake up in the night and think of your work with satisfaction a work at which you would not be ashamed to invoke the Muse.

—Henry David Thoreau

LAUGHTER

As the crackling of thorns under a pot, so is the laughter of the fool.

—Old Testament, Ecclesiastes, VII, 6

Our sincerest laughter
With some pain is fraught.

—Shelley, To a Skylark

You grow up the day you have the first real laugh-at yourself.

—Ethel Barrymore

God hath not granted to woeful mortals even laughter without tears.

—Callimachus

No man who has once heartily and wholly laughed can be altogether and irreclaimably depraved.

—Thomas Carlyle

Laughter is the tonic, the relief, the surcease for pain.

—Charlie Chaplin

You no doubt laugh in your sleeve.

—Cicero

As the crackling of thorns under a pot, so is the laughter of a fool.

—Ecclesiastes 7:6

The loud laugh that spoke the vacant mind.

—Oliver Goldsmith

Laughter unquenchable arose among the blessed gods.

—Homer

Laughing is the sensation of feeling good all over, and showing it principally in one spot.

—Bob Hope

I laugh because I must not cry.

—Abraham Lincoln

Woe unto you that laugh now! For ye shall mourn and weep.

—Luke 6:25

There are three things which are real: God, human folly, and laughter. Since the first two pass our comprehension, we must do what we can with the third.

—Aubrey Menen

LIFE

Gosh! I feel like a real good cry!
Life, he says, is a cheat, a fake.
Well, I agree with the grouchy guy—
The best you get is an even break,

—Franklin P. Adams, *Ballade of Schopenhauer's Philosophy*

If life worth living? That depends on the liver.

—Anon. (c. 1855)

And we are here as on a darkling plain
Swept with confused alarms of struggle and flight,
Where ignorant armies clash by night.

—Matthew Arnold, *Dover Beach*

Why should there be such turmoil and such strife,
To spin in length this feeble line of life?

—Bacon, Translation of Psalm XC

Life! we've "been long together
Through pleasant and through cloudy weather;
Tis hard to part when friends are dear,—
Perhaps 't will cost a sigh, a tear;
Then steal away, give little warning,
Choose thine own time;
Say not "Good Night," but in some brighter clime
Bid me "Good morning."

—Anna L. Barbauld, *Life*

I count life just a stuff to try the soul's strength on.

—R. Browning, *In a Balcony*

I took one draught of life,
I'll tell you what I paid,

Precisely an existence—
The market—price, they said.
—Emily Dickinson, *Further Poems*

They are not long, the weeping and the laughter,
Love and desire and hate:
I think they have no portion in us after
We pass the gate,
—Ernest Dowson, *Vitae Summa BrevisI*

When I consider Life, 'tis all a cheat.
Yet fool'd with hope, men favour the deceit;
Trust on, and think tomorrow will repay.
Tomorrow's falser than the former day;
—Dryden. *Aureng—Zebe, IV, I*

Life ain't all beer and skittles, and more's the pity;
but what's the odds, so long as you're happy?
—George Du Maurier, *Trilby*

A crust of bread and a corner to sleep in,
A minute to smile and an hour to weep in,
A pint of joy to a peck of trouble,
And never a laugh but the moans come double;
And that is lifel
—Paul Laurence Dunbar, *Life*

Life is a jest, and all things show it;
I thought so once, but now I know it,
—John Gay, *My Own Epitaph*

Far from the madding crowd's ignoble strife,
Their sober wishes never learn'd to stray;
Along the cool, sequester'd vale of life
They kept the noiseless tenor of their way,
—Gray, *Elegy Written in a Country Churchyard*

Life is made up of sobs, sniffles, and smiles, with sniffles predominating.

—O. Henry, Gift *of the Magi*

Like leaves on trees the race of man is found,
Now green in youth, now with'ring on the ground:
Another race the following spring supplies,
They fall successive and successive rise.

—Homer, *Iliad, VI* (Pope trans.)

Happy the man, and happy he alone,
He who can call to—day his own:
He who, secure within, can say:
"To—morrow do thy worst, for I have liv'd to—day."

—Horace, *Odes, III, 29* (Dryden trans.)

Welcome, O life! I go to encounter for the millionth time reality of experience and to forge in the smithy of my ! the uncreated conscience of my race.

—James Joyce, *Portrait of the Artist as a Young Man*

The weariness, the fever, and the fret
Here, where men sit and hear each other groan.

—Keats, *Ode to a Nightingale*

I have fought my fight, I have lived my life,
I have drunk my share of wine;
From Trier to Coin there was never a knight
Led a merrier life than mine.

—Charles Kingsley, *The Knight's Leap*

Life is real! Life is earnest!
And the grave is not its goal.

—Longfellow, A *Psalm of Life*

Our ingress into the world
Was naked and bare;
Our progress through the world
Is trouble and care;
Our egress from the world
Will be nobody knows where:
But if we do well here
We shall do well there.

—Longfellow, *Cobbler of Hagenau*

Tell me not in mournful numbers
Life is 'but an empty dream!'
For the soul is dead that slumbers,
And things are not what they seem,

—Longfellow, A *Psalm of Life*

Tomorrow will I live, the fool does say;
Today itself s too late; the wise lived yesterday.

—Martial, *Epigrams,* (Cowley trans.)

Life can be bitter to the very bone
When one is poor, and woman, and alone.

—John Masefield, *The Widow in the Bye Street*

Degenerate sons and daughters,
Life is too strong for you—It takes life to love Life.

—E. L. Masters, Spoon *River Anthology: Lucinda Mattock*

For what is your life? It is even a vapour, that appeareth for a little time, and then vanisheth away,

—New Testament, *James, IV, 14*

As for man his days are as grass: as a flower of the field, so he flourisheth.
The wind passeth over it, and it is gone; and the place thereof shall know it no more.

—Old Testament, *Psalms, CIII, 15,16*

Life is just one damned thing after another,

—Frank Ward O'malley (authorship disputed)

Ah, make the most of what we yet may spend,
Before we too into the Dust descend;
Dust unto Dust, and under Dust to lie,
Sans Wine, sans Song, sans Singer, and—sans End!

—Omar Khayyam, *Rubdiyat* (FitzGerald trans.)

'Strange interlude! Yes, our lives are merely strange dark interludes in the electrical display of God the Father!

—Eugene O'neill, *Strange Interlude*

A little pain, a little pleasure,
A little heaping up of treasure;
Then no more gazing upon the sun.
All things must end that have begun,

—John Payne, *Kyrelle*

Life is adventure in experience, and when you are no longer greedy for the lust drop of it, it means no more than that you have set your face ... to the day when you shall depart, ...

—Donald C. Peattie, *An Almanac for Moderns*

What trifling coil do we poor mortals keep;
Wake, eat and drink, evacuate and sleep.

—Prior, *Human Life*

When I consider Life and its few years—

A wisp of fog betwixt us and the sun;
A call to battle, and the battle done
Ere the last echo dies within our ears;
A rose choked in the grass; an hour of fears;
The gusts that past a darkening shore do beat;
The burst of music down an unlistening street—
I wonder at the idleness of tears.

—Lizette W. Reese, *Tears*

Our past is clean forgot,
Our present is and is not,
Our future's a sealed seedplot,
And what betwixt them are we?

—D. G. Rossetti, The *Cloud Confines*

Life is not a spectacle or a feast; it is a predicament.

—George Santayana, *Articles and Essays*

Life's but a walking shadow, a poor player
That struts and frets his hour upon the stage
And then is heard no more: it is a tale
Told by an idiot, full of sound and fury,
Signifying nothing—

—Shakespeare. *Macbeth. V 5*

We are such stuff
As dreams are made on and our little life
Is rounded with a sleep.

—Shakespeare, *The Tempest, IV, 1*

Life like a dome of many—coloured glass
Stains the white radiance of Eternity,

—Shelley, *Adonais*

From too much love of living,

From hope and fear set free,
We thank with brief thanksgiving
Whatever gods there be,
That no life lives forever;
That dead men rise up never;
That even the weariest river
Winds somewhere safe to sea,

—Swinburne, *The Garden of Proserpine*

And the wild regrets and the bloody sweats
None knew so well as I:
For he who lives more lives than one
More deaths than one must die,

—Oscar Wilde, *Ballad of Reading Gaol*

My life is like the autumn leaf
That trembles in the moon's pale ray;
Its hold is frail—its date is brief,
Restless,—and soon to pass away,

—Richard Henry Wilde, *My Life*

Age and youth look upon life from the opposite ends of the telescope; to the one it is exceedingly long, to the other exceedingly short.

—Henry Ward Beecher

All of the animals, excepting man, know that the principal business of life is to enjoy it.

—Samuel Butter

Life is a test and this world a place of trial. Always the problems-or it may be the same problem-will be presented to every generation in different forms.

—Winston Churchill

I have measured out my life with coffee spoons.

—T. S. Eliot

What is life but the angle of vision? A man is measured by the angle at which he looks at objects.

—Ralph Waldo Emerson

The fool, with all his other faults, has this also: he is always getting ready to live.

—Epicurus

Were it offered to my choice, I should have no objection to a repetition of the same life from its beginnings, only asking the advantages authors have in a second edition to correct some faults.

—Benjamin Franklin

... The fullness of life is in the hazards of life. And, at the worst, there is that in us which can turn defeat into victory.

—Edith Hamelton

I think that, as life is action and passion, it is required of a man that he should share the passion and action of his time at peril of being judged not to have lived.

—Oliver Wendell Holmes

Life is a romantic business. It is painting a picture, not doing a sum—but you have to make the romance, and it will come to the question how much fire you have in your belly.

—Oliver Wendell Holmes

The mind that is cheerful at present will have no solicitude for the future, and will meet the bitter occurrences of life with a smile.

—Horace

... the giver of life, who gave it for happiness and not for wretchedness.

—Thomas Jefferson

Yes! Life is a banquet, and most poor sons-of-bitches are starving to death! Live!

—Jerome Lawrence and Robert E. Lee

Unrest of spirit is a mark of life; one problem after another presents itself and in the solving of them we can find our greatest pleasure.

—Karl Menninger

Life is not so important as the duties of life.

—John Randolph

I wish to preach, not the doctrine of ignoble ease, but the doctrine of the strenuous life.

—Theodore Roosevelt

A baby is God's opinion that life should go on.

—Carl Sandburg

Life is neither a good nor an evil; it is simply the place where good and evil exist.

—Seneca

Life is as tedious as a twice—told tale, Vexing the dull ear of a drowsy man.

—Shakespeare

One man in his time plays many parts, His acts being seven ages.

—Shakespeare

The web of our life is of a mingled yam, good and ill together.

—Shakespeare

Anyone can carry his burden, however hard, until nightfall. Anyone can do his work, however hard, for one day. Anyone can live sweetly, patiently, lovingly, purely, till the sun goes down. And this is all that life really means.

—Attributed to Robert Louis Stevenson

If a man is alive, there is always danger that he may die, though the danger must be allowed to be less in proportion as he is dead and alive to begin with. A man sits as many risks as he runs.

—Henry David Thoreau

LOVE

It is good to be merry and wise,
It is good to be honest and true;
Tis well to be off with the old love
Before you go on with the new,

—Anon. (modern version of an old song)

It's love, it's love that makes the world go round.

—Anon. (used by W, S. Gilbert in *lolanthe*)

Ask not of me, love, what is love?
Ask what is. good of God above—
Ask of the great sun what is light—
Ask what is darkness of the night—
… … … … … … … … … … …
Ask what is sweetness of thy kiss—
Ask of thyself what beauty is.

—P. J. Bailey, *Festas*

For love is of sae mickle might,
That it all paines makis light.

—John Barbour, *The Bruce*

O Happy race of men, if love, which rules Heaven, rule your

minds.

—Boethius, *Consolations of Philosophy*

The night has a thousand eyes,
And the day but one;
Yet the light of the bright world dies
With the dying sun,
The mind has a thousand eyes,
And the heart but one;
Yet the light of a whole life dies
When love is done,

—F. W, Bourdillon, *Light*

Flower o' the broom,
Take away love, and our earth is a tomb!
… … … … … … … … … … … …
Flower o' the clove,
All the Latin I construe is "amo," I love!

—R. Browning, *Fra Lippo Lippi*

O lyric Love, half angel and half bird,
And all a wonder and a wild desire!

—R. Browning, *The Ring and the Book, 1*

Love is the business of the idle, but the idleness of the busy.

—Bulwer-lytton, *Rienzi*

Had we never lov'd sae kindly,
Had we never lov'd sae blindly,
Never met, or never parted,
We had ne'er been broken—hearted!

—Burns, *Ae Fond Kiss*

O, my love is like a red, red rose

That's newly sprung in June.
O, my luve is like the melodie
That's sweetly play'd in tune,
—Burns, *A Red, Red Rose*

The wisest man the warl' e'er saw,
He dearly lov'd the lasses, O.
—Burns, *Green Grow the Rashes.*

To see her is to love her,
And love but her forever;
For nature made her what she is,
And ne'er made sic anither!
—Burns, *O, Saw Ye Bonnie Lesley*

In her first passion woman loves her lover;
In all the others, all she loves is love.
—Byron, *Don Juan, III*

Man's love is of mans life a thing apart,
Tis woman's whole existence,
—Byron, *Don Juan, I*

He that loves a rosy cheek,
Or a coral lip admires,
Or from star—like eyes doth seek:
Fuel to maintain his fires,
As Old Time makes these decay,
So his flames must waste away.
—Thomas Carew, *Disdain Returned*

Let us live, my Lesbia, and love, and value at a penny all the talk of

crabbed old men.
(Vivamus, mea Lesbia atque amemus, ...)
—Catullus, *Odes. V, 1*

For ever it was, and ever it shall befal
That Love is he that alle thing may bind.
—Chaucer, Troilus *and Criseyde, I*

All thoughts, all passions, all delights,
Whatever stirs this mortal frame,
Are but the ministers of Love,
And feed his sacred flame,
—S. T. Coleridge, *Love*

With all thy faults, I love thee still,
—Cowper, The *Task, II*

Oh, I'm in love with the janitor's boy,
And the janitor's boy loves me;
He's going to hunt for a desert isle
In our geography.
—Nathalia Crane, *The Janitor's Boy*

All for Love, or the World Well Lost,
—Dryden, Title of play on theme of *Antony and Cleopatra*

Perhaps they were right in putting love into books, ... Perhaps it could not live anywhere else.
—William Faulkner, *Light in August*

There is a lady sweet and kind,
Was never face so pleased my mind;
I did but see her passing by,
And yet I love her till I die,
—Barnabe Googe, *There Is a Lady (I570)*

He who for the first time loves,

Even vainly, is a God.
But the man who loves again,
And still vainly, is a fool,

—Heine, *Wer zum erstenmale liebt*

You say to me—wards your affection's strong;
Pray love me little, so you love me long.

—Herrick, *Love Me Little, Love Me Long*

Ah! a man's love is strong
When fain he comes a—mating.
But a woman's love is long
And grows when it is waiting,

—Laurence Housman, *The Two Loves*

And, happy melodist, unwearied,
For ever piping songs for ever new;
More happy love! more happy, happy love!
For ever warm and still to be enjoy'd,
For ever panting and for ever young.

—Keats, *Ode on a Grecian Urn*

No longer could I doubt him true—
All other men may use deceit;
He always said my eyes were blue,
And often swore my lips were sweet,

—Landor, *Mother, I Cannot Mind My Wheel*

There are many people who would never have been in love they had never heard love spoken of.

—La Rochefoucauld, *Maxims, 136*

Come live with me and be my Love,
And we will all the pleasures prove

That hills and valleys, dale and field,
Or woods, or steepy mountains yield

—Marlowe, *The Passionate Shepherd to His Love*

Who ever lov'd, that lov'd not at first sight!

—Marlowe, *Hero and Leander I*

Love is all in fire, and yet is ever freezing;
Love is much in winning, yet is more in leesing:
Love is ever sick, and yet is never dying;
Love is ever true, and yet is ever lying;
Love does doat in liking, and is mad in loathing;
Love indeed is anything, yet indeed is nothing.

—Thomas Middleton, *Blurt, 11, 2*

And if I loved you Wednesday,
Well, what is that to you?
I do not love you Thursday—
So much is true,

—Edna St. Vincent Millay, *Thursday*

There's nothing half so sweet in life
As love's young dream.

—Thomas Moore, *Love's Young Dream*

Two souls with but a single thought,
Two hearts that beat as one.

—Von Munch-Bellinghausen, *Ingomar the Barbarian* (Maria A, Lovell, trans.)

Thy love to me was wonderful, passing the love of women

—Old Testament, *II Samuel, I,26*

It was many and many a year ago,
In a Kingdom by the sea,

That a maiden there lived whom you may know
By the name of Annabel Lee;
And this maiden she lived with no other thought
Than to love and be loved by me.
—Poe, *Annabel Lee*

Though his suit was rejected,
He sadly reflected,
That a lover forsaken
A new love may get;
But a neck that's once broken
Can never be set
—Scott, *Peveril of the Peak*

But love is blind, and lovers cannot see
The pretty follies that themselves commit.
—Shakespeare, *Merchant of Venice,II,6*

Doubt thou the stars are fire;
Doubt that the sun doth move;
Doubt truth to be a liar;
But never doubt I love,
—Shakespeare, *Hamlet*

Love is a smoke raised with the fume of sighs:
Being purged, a tire sparkling in lovers' eyes;
Being vex'd, a sea nourish'd with lovers' tears:
What is it else? a madness most discreet,
A choking gall and persevering sweet,
—Shakespeare, *Romeo and Juliet, II, 1*

Men have died from time to time and worms have eaten them, but not for love.

—Shakespeare. *As You Like It, IV, 1*

Sigh no more, ladies, sigh no more,
Men were deceivers ever,
One foot in sea and one on shore,
To one thing constant never.

—Shakespeare, *Much Ado About Nothing, II, 3*

When my love swears that she is made of truth,
I do believe her, though I know she lies.

—Shakespeare, Sonnets, CXXXVIII

When the lamp is shattered
The light in the dust lies dead—
When the cloud is scattered
The rainbow's glory is shed.
When the lute is broken,
Sweet notes are remembered not;
When the lips have spoken,
Loved accents are soon forgot.

—Shelley, *When the Lamp Is Shattered*

Across the gateway of my heart
I wrote "No Thoroughfare,"
But love came laughing by, and cried:
"I enter everywhere."

—Herbert Shipman, *No Thoroughfare*

Out upon it! I have lov'd
Three whole days together;
And am like to love three more,
If it prove fair weather.

—Suckling, *The Constant Lover*

If love were what the rose is,
And I were like the leaf,

Our lives would grow together
In sad or singing weather.

—Swinburne, A *Match*

I hold it true, whate'er befall;
I feel it, when I sorrow most;
Tis better to have loved and lost
Than never to have loved at all,

—Tennyson. *In Memoriam, XXVII*

To say that you can love one person all your life is just like saying that one candle will continue burning as long as you live.

—Tolstoy, *The Kreutzer Sonata*

Love conquers all; let us too yield to Love.
(Omnia vincit Amor; et nos cedamus Amori.)

—Virgil, *Eclogues, X*

Oh, rank is good, and gold is fair,
And high and low mate ill;
But love has never known a law
Beyond its own sweet will!

—Whittier, *Amy Wentworth*

Yet each man kills the thing he loves,
By each let this be heard,
Some do it with a bitter look,
Some with a flattering word,
The coward does it with a kiss,
The brave man with a sword!

—Oscar Wilde, *Ballad* of *Reading Gaol*

I loved a lass, a fair one,
As fair as e'er was seen;

She was indeed a rare one,
Another Sheba queen;
But, fool as then I was,
I thought she loved me too:
But now, alas! she's left me,
Falero, lero, loo!

—George Wither, *The Lover's Resolution*

True love is eternal, infinite, and always like itself. It is equal and pure, without violent demonstrations: it is seen with white hairs and is always young in the heart.

—Honoré de Balzac

How do I love thee? Let me count the ways.
I love thee with a love I seemed to lose
With my lost saints, —I love thee with the breath,
Smiles, tears, of all my life! —If God choose,
I shall but love thee better after death.

—Elizabeth B. Browning

God be thanked, the meanest of his creatures
Boasts two soul—sides, one to face the world with,
One to show a woman when he loves her.

—Robert Browning

Alas! The love of women! It is known To be a lovely and a fearful thing.

—Lord Byron

Love and war are the same thing, and stratagems and policy are as allowable in the one as in the other.

—Cervantes

If love be good, from whennes comth my wo?

—Geoffrey Chaucer

The Stoics define love as the endeavor to form a friendship inspired by beauty.

—Cicero

When povertie comes in at doores, love leaps out at windowes.

—John Clark

Say what you will, 'tis better to be left Than never to have loved.

—William Congreve

We are all born for love ... It is the principle of existence and its only end.

—Benjamin Disraeli

But you must believe me when I tell you that I have found it impossible to carry the heavy burden of responsibility and to discharge my duties as King as I would wish to do without the help and support of the woman I love.

—Edward VIII

All mankind love a lover.

—Ralph Waldo Emerson

He is not a lover who does not love forever.

—Euripides

For, you see, each day I love you more,
Today more than yesterday and less than tomorrow.

—Rosemonde Gérard

Love has power that dispels Death; charm that conquers the enemy.

—Kahlil Gibran

Love grants in a moment
What toil can hardly achieve in an age.

—Goethe

Ah! What is love?
It is a pretty thing,
As sweet unto a shepherd as a king,
And sweeter too;
For kings have cares that wait upon a crown,
And cares can make the sweetest love to frown.

—Robert Greene

To demand of love that it be without jealousy is to ask of light that it cast no shadows.

—Oscar Hammling

All brave men love; for he only is brave who has affections to fight for, whether in the daily battle of life, or in physical contests.

—Nathaniel Hawthorne

If you would be loved, love.

—Hecato

Who love too much, hate in the like extreme.

—Homer

A women is more considerate in affairs of love than a man; because love is more the study and business of her life.

—Washington Irving

Greater love hath no man than this, that a man lay down his life for his friends.

—John 15:13

There is no fear in love; but perfect love casteth out fear.

—I John 4:8

Love in a hut, with water and a crust,
Is—love, forgive ust—cinders, ashes, dust.

—John Keats

Come live with me and be my love,
And we will all the pleasures prove,
That valleys, groves, or hills, or fields,
Or woods and steepy mountains yields.

—Christopher Marlowe

'Tis not love's going hurts my days,
But that it went in little ways.

—Edna St. Vincent Millay

Take love away from life and you take away its pleasures.

—Molière

'Tis sweet to think, that, where'er we rove,
We are sure to find something blissful and dear;
And when we're far from the lips we love,
We've but to make love to the lips we are near.

—Thomas Moore

Love is indeed heaven upon earth; since heaven above would not be heaven without it; ...

—William Penn

If all the world and love were young,
And truth in every shepherd's tongue,
These pretty pleasures might me move
To live with thee, and be thy love.

—Sir Walter Raleigh

The pleasure of love is in loving; and we are much happier in the passion we feel than in that which we inspire.

—François de la Rochefoucauld

Whither thou goest, I will go; and where thou lodgest, I will lodge: thy people shall be my people, and thy God my God.

—Ruth 1:16

No sooner met but they looked, no sooner looked but they loved, no sooner loved but they sighed, no sooner sighed but they asked one another the reason.

—Shakespeare

Where love is great, the littlest doubts are fear;
When little fears grow great, great love grows there.

—Shakespeare

But love is blind, and lovers cannot see
The pretty follies that themselves commit.

—Shakespeare

Ay me! for aught that I ever could read,
Could ever hear by tale or history,
The course of true love never did run smooth.

—Shakespeare

Speak low, if you speak love.

—Shakespeare

There is no creature loves me,
And if I die, no soul shall pity me.

—Shakespeare

First love is only a little foolishness and a lot of curiosity: no really self—respecting woman would take advantage of it.

—George Bernard Shaw

Love is a symbol of eternity. It wipes out all sense of time, destroying all memory of a beginning and all fear of an end.

—Madame de Stetl

And blessings on the falling out
That all the more endears,
When we fall out with those we love,

And kiss again with tears.

—Alfred, Lord Tennyson

To say that you can love one person all your life is just like saying that one candle will continue burning as long as you live.

—Leo Tolstoy

Beware of her fair locks, for when she winds them round a young man's neck, she will not set him free again.

—Johann Wolfgang von Goethe

MISCELLANEOUS

The body is a house of many windows: there we all sit, showing ourselves and crying on the passers—by to come and love us.

—Robert Louis Stevenson

I remembered a story of how Bach was approached by a young admirer one day and asked, "But Papa Bach, how do you manage to think of all these new tunes?" "My dear fellow," Bach is said to have answered, according to my version, "I have no need to think of them. I have the greatest difficulty not to step on them when I get out of bed in the morning and start moving around my room."

—Laurens Van der Post

I'm afraid that if you look at a thing long enough, it loses all of its meaning.

—Andy Warhol

Nothing so much prevents our being natural as the desire to seem so.

—François, Duc de La Rochefoucauld, *Maxims*, 1678

It wasn't raining when Noah built the ark.

—Howard Ruff, *How to Prosper in the Coming Bad Years*, 1979

He that hath the name to be an early riser may sleep till noon.

—James Howell, *Proverbs*, 1659

A variety of nothing is superior to a monotony of something.

—Johann Paul Friedrich Richter

You can never plan the future by the past.

—Edmund Burke, "*Letter to a Member of the National Assembly*"

Possessions are usually diminished by possession.

—Friedrich Wilhelm Nietzsche, *The Gay Science*

After all, the main question will be the opener: "Hello, are you there?" If the reply should turn out to be "Yes, hello," we might want to stop there and think about that, for quite a long time.

—Lewis Thomas, *Lives of a Cell*, 1974

Human beings, vegetables, or cosmic dust — we all dance to a mysterious tune, intoned in the distance by an invisible piper.

—Albert Einstein, in *The Saturday Evening Post*, 26 October 1929

Coincidence is God's way of remaining anonymous.

—Albert Einstein

We are the products of editing, rather than authorship.

—George Wald, "The Origin of Optical Activity," *Annals of the New York Academy of Science*, 1975

All our scientific and philosophic ideals are altars to unknown gods.

—William James, *The Dilemma of Determinism*, 1884

House, *n*: A hollow edifice erected for the habitation of man, rat, mouse, beetle, cockroach, fly, mosquito, flea, bacillus, and microbe.

—Ambrose Bierce, *The Devil's Dictionary*

I can live with doubt and uncertainty. I think it's much more interesting to live not knowing than to have answers which might be wrong.

—Richard P. Feynman

My own suspicion is that the universe is not only queerer than we suppose, but queerer than we can suppose.

—J.B.S. Haldane, *Possible Worlds and Other Papers*, 1927

I simply believe that some part of the human Self or Soul is not subject to the laws of space and time.

—Carl Jung

The universe is full of magical things, patiently waiting for our wits to grow sharper.

—Eden Phillpotts, *A Shadow Passes*

The best things said come last. People will talk for hours saying nothing much and then linger at the door with words that come with a rush from the heart.

—Alan Alda

If ifs were gifts, every day would be Christmas.

—Charles Barkley

That guy has muscles in places most people don't have places.

—Bucky Waters, on Tom Hammonds

In small proportions we just beauties see,
And in short measures life may perfect be.

—Ben Jonson, *To the Immortal Memory and Friendship of that Noble Pair, Sir Lucius Cary and Sir H. Morison*, 1640

Perfect behavior is born of complete indifference.

—Cesare Pavese, *This Business of Living: Diaries*

Our virtues and vices couple with one another, and get children that resemble both their parents.

—George Savile, Marquess de Halifax, *Miscellaneous Thoughts and Reflections*

The most decisive actions of our life ... are most often unconsidered actions.

—André Gide, *The Counterfeiters*, 1926

It is not impossibilities which fill us with the deepest despair, but possibilities which we have failed to realize.

—Robert Mallett, *Apostilles*, 1972

In skating over thin ice, our safety is in our speed.

—Ralph Waldo Emerson

Every truth passes through three stages before it is recognized. In the first, it is ridiculed, in the second it is opposed, in the third it is regarded as self—evident.

—Arthur Schopenhauer

Our greatest pretenses are built up not to hide the evil and the ugly in us, but our emptiness. The hardest thing to hide is something that is not there.

—Eric Hoffer, *Passionate State of Mind*, 1955

It's pretty hard to be efficient without being obnoxious.

—Kin Hubbard

Any philosophy that can be put in a nutshell belongs there.

—Branch Rickey

Now he has departed from this strange world a little ahead of me. That signifies nothing. For us believing physicists the distinction between past, present, and future is only a stubbornly persistent illusion.

—Albert Einstein

God made everything out of nothing. But the nothingness shows through.

—Paul Valéry, *Mauvaises pensées et autres*, 1942

It is better to waste one's youth than to do nothing with it at all.

—Georges Courteline, *La philosophie de Georges Courteline*, 1917

It is impossible to win gracefully at chess. No man has yet said "Mate!" in a voice which failed to sound to his opponent bitter, boastful and malicious.

—A.A. Milne, *Not That It Matters*, 1919

Doubt is not a pleasant state of mind, but certainty is absurd.

—Voltaire, 1767

We're all hookers. What matters is dignity.

—Mike Farren

We dance round in a ring and suppose,
But the Secret sits in the middle and knows.

—Robert Frost, *In the Clearing*, 1962

The ideas I stand for are not mine. I borrowed them from Socrates. I swiped them from Chesterfield. I stole them from Jesus. And I put them in a book. If you don't like their rules, whose would you use?

—Dale Carnegie

Passion is universal humanity. Without it religion, history, romance and art would be useless.

—Honoré de Balzac

Convictions are more dangerous enemies of truth than lies.

—Friedrich Wilhelm Nietzsche, *Human, All Too Human*, 1878

Two roads diverged in a wood, and I —
I took the one less traveled by,
And that has made all the difference.

—Robert Frost, "*The Road Not Taken*," 1916

No matter what happens ... somebody will find a way to take it too seriously.

—Dave Barry, "*Things That It Took Me 50 Years to Learn*"

Architecture begins where engineering ends.

—Walter Gropius

I've got dreams in hidden places and extra smiles for when I'm blue.

—Author Unknown

I believe in rules. Sure I do. If there weren't any rules, how could you break them?

—Leo Durocher

You never know till you try to reach them how accessible men are; but you must approach each man by the right door.

—Henry Ward Beecher, *Proverbs from Plymouth Pulpit*, 1887

Keep a diary and one day it'll keep you.

—Mae West

He is a true fugitive who flies from reason.

—Marcus Aurelius

A wise man is not governed by others, nor does he try to govern them; he prefers that reason alone prevail.

—La Bruyère, *Characters*, 1688

The last function of reason is to recognize that there are an infinity of things which surpass it.

—Blaise Pascal, *Pensées*, 1670

All man's troubles come from not knowing how to sit still in one room.

—Blaise Pascal, *Pensées*, 1670

Saint, *n*: A dead sinner revised and edited.

—Ambrose Bierce, *The Devil's Dictionary*, 1911

All my best thoughts were stolen by the ancients.

—Ralph Waldo Emerson

And thus I clothe my naked villainy
With odd old ends stolen forth of Holy Writ
And seem a saint when most I play the devil.

—William Shakespeare, *Richard III*, 1593

From the satisfaction of desire there may arise, accompanying joy and as it were sheltering behind it, something not unlike despair.

—André Gide, *The Counterfeiters*, 1925

A scholar who loves comfort is not fit to be called a scholar.

—Confucius, *Analects*

There is nothing noble about being superior to some other person. The true nobility is in being superior to your previous self.

—Hindustani Proverb

Truth is tough. It will not break, like a bubble, at a touch, nay, you may kick it all about all day like a football, and it will be round and full at evening.

—Oliver Wendell Holmes, *The Professor at the Breakfast Table*

To live is in itself a value judgment. To breathe is to judge.

—Albert Camus, *The Rebel*, 1951

Virtue is an angel, but she is a blind one, and must ask Knowledge to show her the pathway that leads to her goal.

—Horace Mann, "*Thoughts for a Young Man*," 1859

Virtue is praised, but hated. People run from it, for it is ice—cold and in this world you have to keep your feet warm.

—Denis Diderot, *Rameau's Nephew*, 1762

No man sees far; the most see no farther than their noses.

—Thomas Carlyle, "*Count Cagliostro*," 1833

Revolutions are not made: they come. A revolution is as natural as an oak tree. It comes out of the past; its foundations are laid far back.

—Wendell Phillips, *Address, Anti-Slavery Society*, 1852

The reward of a thing well done is to have done it.

—Emerson, *Essays: Second Series*, 1844

From a worldly point of view there is no mistake so great as that of being always right.

—Samuel Butler, *Note-Books*, 1912

I say *me*, knowing all the while it's not me.

—Samuel Beckett, *The Unnamable*, 1953

What other dungeon is so dark as one's own heart! What jailer so inexorable as one's self.

—Nathaniel Hawthorne, *The House of Seven Gables*, 1822

He who is allowed to do as he likes will soon run his head into a brick wall out of sheer frustration.

—Robert Musil, *The Man without Qualities*, 1930

Some minds seem almost to create themselves, springing up under every disadvantage and working their solitary but irresistible way through a thousand obstacles.

—Washington Irving, *The Sketch Book*, 1820

A play should give you something to think about. When I see a play and understand it the first time, then I know it can't be much good.

—T.S. Eliot, *New York Post*, 22 September 1963

Theory helps us bear our ignorance of facts.

—George Santayana, *The Sense of Beauty*, 1896

It is better to emit a scream in the shape of a theory than to be entirely insensible to the jars and incongruities of life and take everything as it comes in a forlorn stupidity.

—Robert Louis Stevenson, "Crabbed Age and Youth," *Virginibus Puerisque*, 1881

Thoughts, like fleas, jump from man to man. But they don't bite everybody.

—Stanislaw Lec, *Unkempt Thoughts*, 1962

The thoughts that come often unsought, and, as it were, drop into the mind, are commonly the most valuable of any we have.

—John Locke, 16 May 1699

True generosity consists precisely in fighting to destroy the causes which nourish false charity.

—Paulo Freire, *Pedagogy of the Oppressed*, 1970

Biographies are but the clothes and buttons of the man — the biography of the man himself cannot be written.

—Mark Twain, *Autobiography*, 1924

There is no such thing as a moral or immoral book; books are well written or badly written.

—Oscar Wilde, *Picture of Dorian Gray*, 1891

A "fraternity" is the antithesis of *fraternity*. The first ... is predicated on the idea of exclusion; the second (that is, the abstract thing) is based on a feeling of total equality.

—E.B. White, *One Man's Meat*, 1944

While there is a lower class I am in it, while there is a criminal element I am of it; while there is a soul in prison, I am not free.

—Eugene V. Debs, Cleveland, 1917

We cannot bear to regard ourselves simply as playthings of blind chance; we cannot admit to feeling ourselves abandoned.

—Ugo Betti, *Struggle till Dawn*, 1949

People seem not to see that their opinion of the world is also a confession of character.

—Emerson, *The Conduct of Life*, 1860

We confess to little faults only to persuade ourselves that we have no great ones.

—François, Duc de La Rochefoucauld, *Maxims*, 1665

Men never do evil so thoroughly and cheerfully as when they do it for conscience sake.

—Blaise Pascal, *Pensées*, 1670

The study of crime begins with the knowledge of oneself.

—Henry Miller, *The Air-Conditioned Nightmare*, 1945

We learn geology the morning after the earthquake.

—Ralph Waldo Emerson, *The Conduct of Life*, 1860

Let's not forget that the little emotions are the great captains of our lives and we obey them without realizing it.

—Vincent Van Gogh, 1889

The sinning is the best part of repentance.

—Arab Proverb

Most people die at the last minute; others twenty years beforehand, some even earlier. They are the wretched of the earth.

—Louis Céline, *Voyage au bout du monde*, 1932

Most men are more capable of great actions than of good ones.

—Montesquieu, *Variètès*

Some defeats [are] more triumphant than victories.

—Montaigne, *Essays*, 1588

The passion to get ahead is sometimes born of the fear lest we be left behind.

—Eric Hoffer, *The Passionate State of Mind*, 1954

In every age "the good old days" were a myth. No one ever thought they were good at the time. For every age has consisted of crises that seemed intolerable to the people who lived through them.

—Brooks Atkinson, *Once Around the Sun*, 1951

They ... who await
No gifts from Chance, have conquered Fate.

—Matthew Arnold, "*Resignation*," 1849

Misfortunes one can endure — they come from outside, they are accidents. But to suffer for one's own faults — ah! there is the sting of life.

—Oscar Wilde, *Lady Windermere's Fan*, 1892

It takes more strength of character to withstand good fortune than bad.

—La Rochefoucauld, *Reflections*, 1665

The right to be heard does not automatically include the right to be taken seriously.

—Hubert Humphrey, speech, Madison, Wisconsin, 23 August 1965

The future is called "perhaps," which is the only possible thing to call the future.

—Tennessee Williams, *Orpheus Descending*, 1957

I believe the future is only the past again, entered through another gate.

—Arthur Wing Pinero, *The Second Mrs. Tanqueray*, 1893

Do not do unto others as you would that they should do unto you. Their tastes may not be the same.

—G.B. Shaw, "*Maxims for Revolutionists*," 1898

No man is truly great who is great only in his own lifetime. The test of greatness is the page of history.

—William Hazlitt, *Table Talk*, 1822

I think the enemy is here before us.... I think the enemy is simple selfishness and compulsive greed.... I think he stole our earth from us, destroyed our wealth, and ravaged and despoiled our land.

—Thomas Wolfe, *You Can't Go Home Again*, 1949

There is a sort of man who pays no attention to his good actions, but is tormented by his bad ones. This is the type that most often writes about himself.

—W. Somerset Maugham, *The Summing Up*, 1938

I find my joy of living in the fierce and ruthless battles of life, and my pleasure comes from learning something.

—Auguste Strindberg, *Miss Julie*, 1888

Every idea I get I have to deny, that's my way of testing it.

—Alain, *Histoire de mes pensées*

Others go to bed with their mistresses; I with my ideas.

—José Marti, letter, 1890

Men are idolaters and want something to look at and kiss and hug, or throw themselves down before; they always did, they always will; and if you don't make it out of wood, you must make it out of words.

—Oliver Wendell Holmes, *The Poet at the Breakfast Table*, 1872

Man has always sacrificed truth to his vanity, comfort and advantage. He lives ... by make-believe.

—W. Somerset Maugham, *The Summing Up*, 1938

We look for some reward of our endeavours and are disappointed; not success, not happiness, not even peace of conscience, crowns our ineffectual efforts to do well.

—Robert Louis Stevenson, "Pulvis et umbra," 1888

Do I contradict myself?
Very well then I contradict myself.
(I am large, I contain multitudes.)

—Walt Whitman, *Leaves of Grass*, 1892

It is human nature to stand in the middle of a thing.

—Mariane Moore, "A Grave," *Collected Poems*, 1951

"Independence" ... [is] middle—class blasphemy. We are all dependent on one another, every soul of us on earth.

—G.B. Shaw, *Pygmalion*, 1912

The whole theory of the universe is directed unerringly to one single individual — namely to You.

—Walt Whitman, *Leaves of Grass*, 1892

To have a grievance is to have a purpose in life.

—Alan Coren, *The Sanity Inspector*, 1974

People wish to be settled: only as far as they are unsettled is there any hope for them.

—Ralph Waldo Emerson, *Essays*, 1841

Say "Yes" to the seedlings and a giant forest cleaves the sky. Say "Yes" to the universe and the planets become your neighbors. Say "Yes" to dreams of love and freedom. It is the password to utopia.

—Brooks Atkinson, *Once Around the Sun*, 1951

The worst of a modern stylish mansion is that it has no place for ghosts.

—Oliver Wendell Holmes, *The Poet at the Breakfast Table*, 1872

The real hero is always a hero by mistake; he dreams of being an honest coward like everybody else.

—Umberto Eco, *Travels in Hyper Reality*, 1986

We owe to the Middle Ages the two worst inventions of humanity — romantic love and gunpowder.

—André Maurois, BBC—TV, January 1958

To say yes, you have to sweat and roll up your sleeves and plunge both hands into life up to the elbows. It is easy to say no, even if saying no means death.

—Jean Anouilh, *Antigone*, 1942

Of all sad words of tongue or pen,
The saddest are these: "It might have been!"

—John Greenleaf Whittier, "Maud Muller," 1854

Any notion of the serious life of leisure, as well as men's taste and capacity to live it, has disappeared. Leisure [has become] entertainment.

—Allan Bloom, *The Closing of the American Mind*, 1987

Not ... *what* opinions are held, but ... *how* they are held: instead of being held dogmatically, [liberal] opinions are held tentatively, and with a consciousness that new evidence may at any moment lead to their abandonment.

—Bertrand Russell, *Unpopular Essays*, 1950

The chief characteristics of the [liberal] attitude are human sympathy, a receptivity to change, and a scientific willingness to follow reason rather than faith.

—Chester Bowles, *New Republic*, 22 July 1946

Liberal institutions straightway cease from being liberal the moment they are soundly established.

—Nietzsche, *Twilight of the Idols*, 1888

The thing I am most aware of is my limits. And this is natural; for I never, or almost never, occupy the middle of my cage; my whole being surges toward the bars.

—André Gide, *Journals*, 4 August 1930

Loyalty in a free society depends upon the toleration of disloyalty.

—Alan Barth, *The Loyalty of Free Man*, 1951

His designs were strictly honorable, as the phrase is: that is, to rob a lady of her fortune by way of marriage.

—Henry Fielding, *Tom Jones*, 1749

Martyrdom has always been a proof of the intensity, never the correctness, of a belief.

—Arthur Schweitzer, *Out of My Life and Thought*, 1932

The absurd is clear reason recognizing its limits.

—Albert Camus, *Le Suicide philosophique*

When to the sessions of sweet silent thought
I summon up remembrance of things past,
I sigh the lack of many a thing I sought
And with old woes new wail my dear times' waste.

—William Shakespeare, *Sonnet No. 30*

The world more often rewards the appearance of merit than merit itself.

—La Rochefoucauld, *Maxims*, 1665

It is not always by plugging away at a difficulty and sticking to it that one overcomes it; often it is by working on the one next to it. Some things and some people have to be approached obliquely, at an angle.

—André Gide, *Journals*, 26 October 1924

The professional military mind is by necessity an inferior and unimaginative mind; no man of high intellectual quality would willingly imprison his gifts in such a calling.

—H.G. Wells, *The Outline of History*, 1920

What is morality in any given time or place? It is what the majority then and there happen to like, and immorality is what they dislike.

—Alfred North Whitehead, *Dialogues*, 30 August 1941

It is not reason that gives us our moral orientation, it is sensitivity.

—Maurice Barreès, *La Grande Pitié des églises de France*, 1914

Many eyes go through the meadow, but few see the flowers in it.

—Ralph Waldo Emerson, *Journals*, 1834

It is easier to believe than to doubt.

—E.D. Martin, *The Meaning of a Liberal Education*

Blessed are the young, for they shall inherit the national debt.

—Herbert Hoover

The high cost of
living isnt so bad if you
dont have to pay for it

—Don Marquis, *Archy and Mehitabel*, 1927

Modern man lives under the illusion that he knows what he wants, while he actually wants what he is supposed to want.

—Erich Fromm, *Escape from Freedom*, 1941

We kill because we are afraid of our own shadow, afraid that if we used a little common sense we'd have to admit that our glorious principles were wrong.

—Henry Miller, *The Wisdom of the Heart*, 1941

We're all born brave, trusting and greedy, and most of us remain greedy.

—Mignon McLaughlin

A small man can be just as exhausted as a great man.

—Arthur Miller

There are some men who, in a fifty-fifty proposition, insist on getting the hyphen, too.

—Author Unknown

Everybody wants to be somebody; nobody wants to grow.

—Johann Wolfgang von Goethe

Wandering seemed no more than the happiness of an anxious man.

—Albert Camus

Rather perish than hate and fear, and twice rather perish than make oneself hated and feared — this must some day become the highest maxim for every single commonwealth.

—Friedrich Nietzsche

What a pity that the only way to heaven is in a hearse.

—Stanislaw J. Lec

The wicked often work harder to go to hell than the righteous do to enter heaven.

—Josh Billings

Ideals are like stars: you will not succeed in touching them with your hands, but like the seafaring man on the desert of waters, you choose them as your guides, and following them you reach your destiny.

—Carl Schurz

Every dogma has its day, but ideals are eternal.

—Israel Zangwill

An idea isn't responsible for the people who believe in it.

—Don Marquis

There is only one way in which a person acquires a new idea: by the combination or association of two or more ideas he already has into a new juxtaposition in such a manner as to discover a relationship among them of which he was not previously aware.

—Francis A. Cartier

The average man, who does not know what to do with his life, wants another one which will last forever.

—Anatole France

The People, though we think of a great entity when we use the word, means nothing more than so many millions of individual men.

—James Bryce

When we lose our individual independence in the corporateness of a mass movement, we find a new freedom — freedom to hate, bully, lie, torture, murder and betray without shame and remorse.

—Eric Hoffer

In all things that are purely social we can be as separate as the fingers, yet one as the hand in all things essential to mutual progress.

—Booker T. Washington

The man who says he is willing to meet you halfway is usually a poor judge of distance.

—Author Unknown

We should all be obliged to appear before a board every five years, and justify our existence ... on pain of liquidation.

—George Bernard Shaw

The new frontier lies not beyond the planets but within each one of us.

—Pierre Elliot Trudeau, *Biodynamics*

It is often wonderful how putting down on paper a clear statement of a case helps one to see, not perhaps the way out, but the way in.

—Arthur Christopher Benson

However mean your life is, meet it and live it; do not shun it and call it hard names. It is not so bad as you are.

—Henry David Thoreau

None are so blind as those who will not see.

—Author Unknown

"But" is a fence over which few leap.

—German Proverb

Dare to be naive.

—Buckminster Fuller

For people who live on expectations, to face up to their realization is something of an ordeal.

—Elizabeth Bowen

When a man does not know what harbor he is making for, no wind is the right wind.

—Seneca

The goal of all civilization, all religious thought, and all that sort of thing is simply to have a good time. But man gets so solemn over the process that he forgets the end.

—Don Marquis

Preach not to others what they should eat, but eat as becomes you and be silent.

—Epictetus

Undoubtedly the desire for food has been and still is one of the main causes of political events.

—Bertrand Russell

Never argue at the dinner table, for the one who is not hungry always gets the best of the argument.

—Richard Whately

A converted cannibal is one who, on Friday, eats only fishermen.

—Emily Lotney

There is more simplicity in the man who eats caviar on impulse than in the man who eats grapenuts on principle.

—G.K. Chesterton

Wine is sure proof that God loves us and wants us to be happy.

—Benjamin Franklin

With what a leaden and retarding weight
Does expectation load the wing of time!

—William Mason

When you reach for the stars, you may not quite get one, but you won't come up with a handful of mud either.

—Leo Burnett

Each has his past shut in him like the leaves of a book shown to him by heart, and his friends can only read the title.

—Virginia Woolf

Give us Lord, a bit o' sun,
A bit o' work and a bit o' fun;
Give us all in the struggle and sputter
Our daily bread and a bit o' butter.

—From an inn in Lancaster, England

Spirituality is ... the awareness that survival is the savage fight between you and yourself.

—Author Unknown

A man needs self-acceptance or he can't live with himself; he needs self-criticism or others can't live with him.

—James A. Pike

Ruin and recovery are both from within.

—Epictetus

Every man is his own ancestor, and every man his own heir. He devises his own future, and he inherits his own past.

—H.F. Hedge

Circumstances are the rulers of the weak; they are but the instruments of the wise.

—Samuel Lover

I am my own heaven and hell!

—J.C.F. von Schiller

To have doubted one's own first principles is the mark of a civilized man.

—Oliver Wendell Holmes, Jr.

The Anglo-Saxon conscience doesn't keep you from doing what you shouldn't; it just keeps you from enjoying it.

—Salvador de Madariaga

A man who is not a Liberal at sixteen has no heart; a man who is not a Conservative at sixty has no head.

—Benjamin Disraeli

The only man who can change his mind is a man that's got one.

—Edward Noyes Westcott

To speak ill of others is a dishonest way of praising ourselves.

—Will and Ariel Durant

I can't say as ever I was lost, but I was bewildered once for three days.

—Daniel Boone

He was a "how" thinker, not an "if" thinker.

—Author Unknown

I hate the giving of the hand unless the whole man accompanies it.

—Ralph Waldo Emerson

To be always ready a man must be able to cut a knot, for everything cannot be untied.

—Henri Frederic Amiel

Nothing reaches the intellect before making its appearance in the senses.

—Latin Proverb

Passion and prejudice govern the world, only under the name of reason.

—John Wesley

Life is not governed by will or intention. Life is a question of nerves, and fibers, and slowly built-up cells in which thought hides itself and passion has its dreams.

—Oscar Wilde

But are not this struggle and even the mistakes one may make better, and do they not develop us more, than if we kept systematically away from emotions?

—Vincent Van Gogh

We are sure to be losers when we quarrel with ourselves; it is civil war.

—Charles Caleb Colton

If Heaven made him — earth can find some use for him.

—Chinese Proverb

Choices are the hinges of destiny.

—Edwin Markham

People "died" all the time.... Parts of them died when they made the wrong kinds of decisions — decisions against life. Sometimes they died bit by bit until finally they were just living corpses walking around. If you were perceptive you could see it in their eyes; the fire had gone out ... you always knew when you made a decision against life.... The door clicked and you were safe inside — safe and dead.

—Anne Morrow Lindbergh

Some persons are very decisive when it comes to avoiding decisions.

—Brendan Francis

If ... you can't be a good example, then you'll just have to be a horrible warning.

—Catherine Aird

One filled with joy preaches without preaching.

—Mother Teresa

We all live under the same sky, but we don't all have the same horizon.

—Konrad Adenauer

Life is like a game of cards. The hand you are dealt is determinism; the way you play it is free will.

—Jawaharial Nehru

There is only one thing about which I am certain, and that is that there is very little about which one can be certain.

—W. Somerset Maugham

Experience taught me a few things. One is to listen to your gut, no matter how good something sounds on paper. The second is that you're generally better off sticking with what you know. And the third is that sometimes your best investments are the ones you don't make.

—Donald Trump

We should all be concerned about the future because we will have to spend the rest of our lives there.

—Charles F. Kettering

You're not dumb, or stupid, just thoroughly wrong.

—Jerry Kopke

The best things in life aren't things.

—Art Buchwald

A man dies still if he has done nothing, as one who has done much.

—Homer

The real problem of leisure time is how to keep others from using yours.

—Arthur Lacey

He enjoys true leisure who has time to improve his soul's estate.

—Henry David Thoreau

Man never has what he wants, because what he wants is everything.

—C.F. Ramuz

I am convinced, the longer I live, that life and its blessings are not so entirely unjustly distributed as when we are suffering greatly we are inclined to suppose.

—Mary Todd Lincoln

To most of us the real life is the life we do not lead.

—Oscar Wilde

Wanting to change, to improve, a person's situation means offering him, for difficulties in which he is practiced and experienced, other difficulties that will find him perhaps even more bewildered.

—Rainer Maria Rilke

Comparison, more than reality, makes men happy or wretched.

—Thomas Fuller

If a man could have just half of his wishes, he would double his troubles.

—Benjamin Franklin

The next best thing to knowing something is knowing where to find it.

—Samuel Johnson

How much has to be explored and discarded before reaching the naked flesh of feeling.

—Claude Debussy

Generally the theories we believe we call facts, and the facts we disbelieve we call theories.

—Felix Cohen

The Arctic expresses the sum of all wisdom: Silence.

—Walter Bauer

Every man has three characters — that which he exhibits, that which he has, and that which he thinks he has.

—Alphonse Karr

Know then thyself, presume not God to scan:
The proper study of mankind is man.

—Alexander Pope, *Essay on Man*, 1733

Much unhappiness results from our inability to remember the nice things that happen to us.

—W.N. Rieger

If we go down into ourselves, we find that we possess exactly what we desire.

—Simone Weil

The greatest evil which fortune can inflict on men is to endow them with small talents and great ambitions.

—Vauvenargues

There is no good in arguing with the inevitable. The only argument available with an east wind is to put on your overcoat.

—James Russell Lowell, *Democracy and Other Addresses*, 1887

To do the useful thing, to say the courageous thing, to contemplate the beautiful thing: that is enough for one man's life.

—T.S. Eliot

It is not how busy you are, but why you are busy — the bee is praised, the mosquito is swatted.

—Author Unknown

Lots of folks confuse bad management with destiny.

—Kin Hubbard

The time will come when winter will ask you what you were doing all summer.

—Henry Clay

The sunrise never failed us yet.

—Celia Thaxter

I know not what the future holds, but I know who holds the future.

—Author Unknown

The only sense we still respect is eyesight, probably because it is so closely attached to the brain. Go into any American house at random, you will find something — a plastic flower, false tiles, some imitation something — something which can be appreciated as material only if apprehended by eyesight alone. Don't we go sightseeing in cars, thinking we can experience a landscape by looking at it through glass?

—Galway Kinnell, *Poetry, Personality and Death*

Bear shame and glory with an equal peace and an ever tranquil heart.

—Bhagavad Gita

Before we set our hearts too much upon anything, let us examine how happy they are, who already possess it.

—François Duc de La Rochefoucauld

Not everything that can be counted counts, and not everything that counts can be counted.

—Albert Einstein

The world is moving so fast these days that the man who says it can't be done is generally interrupted by someone doing it.

—Harry Emerson Fosdick

I dwell in Possibility
A fairer house than Prose
More numerous of Windows
Superior — for Doors.

—Emily Dickinson

If I have seen further it is by standing on the shoulders of Giants.

—Isaac Newton, letter to Robert Hooke, 5 February 1675

Unless we change direction, we are likely to end up where we are going.

—Author Unknown

Tomorrow is the most important thing in life. Comes into us at midnight very clean. It's perfect when it arrives and it puts itself in our hands. It hopes we've learned something from yesterday.

—John Wayne

Sometimes you have to get to know someone really well to realize you're really strangers.

—Mary Tyler Moore

If there's another world, he lives in bliss;
If there is none, he made the best of this.

—Robert Burns, "*Epitaph on William Muir*"

I would prefer not to.

—Herman Melville, "*Bartleby, the Scrivener*"

I am a kind of paranoiac in reverse. I suspect people of plotting to make me happy.

—J.D. Salinger

All she keeps inside isn't on the label.

—Fuel

The greatest evil which fortune can inflict on men is to endow them with small talents and great ambition.

—Luc de Clapiers marquis de Vauvenargues

Passion, though a bad regulator, is a powerful spring.

—Ralph Waldo Emerson

Everyone is a moon, and has a dark side which he never shows to anybody.

—Mark Twain, *Pudd'nhead Wilson*, 1894

The self cannot be escaped, but it can be, with ingenuity and hard work, distracted.

—Donald Barthelme

It's frustrating when you know all the answers, but nobody bothers to ask you the questions.

—Author Unknown

Myths and creeds are heroic struggles to comprehend the truth in the world.

—Ansel Adams

Ideas have become far more important to us than action — ideas so cleverly expressed in books by the intellectuals in every field. The more cunning, the more subtle, those ideas are the more we worship them and the books that contain them. We are those books, we are those ideas, so heavily conditioned are we by them. We are forever discussing ideas and ideals and dialectically offering opinions. Every religion has its dogma, its formula, its own scaffold to reach the gods, and when inquiring into the beginning of thought we are questioning the importance of this whole edifice of ideas. We have separated ideas from action because ideas are always of the past and action is always the present — that is, living is always the present. We are afraid of living and therefore the past, as ideas, has become so important to us.

—J. Krishnamurti

An expert is one who knows more and more about less and less.

—Nicholas Murray Butler

Civilizations have been founded and maintained on theories which refused to obey facts.

—Joe Orton, *What the Butler Saw*, 1969

Only as high as I reach can I grow
Only as far as I seek can I go
Only as deep as I look can I see
Only as much as I dream can I be.

—Karen Ravn

He who has a thousand friends has not a friend to spare, and he who has one enemy will meet him everywhere.

—Ralph Waldo Emerson

Celebrate the happiness that friends are always giving. Make every day a holiday and celebrate just living!

—Amanda Bradley

Discretion is being able to raise your eyebrow instead of your voice.

—Author Unknown

It's like, at the end, there's this surprise quiz: am I proud of me? I gave my life to become the person I am right now! Was it worth what I paid?

—Richard Bach

Whatever you are be a good one.

—Abraham Lincoln

Don't let anyone steal your dream. It's your dream, not theirs.

—Dan Zadra

There is a fine line between dreams and reality, it's up to you to draw it.

—B. Quilliam

Grow old with me! The best is yet to be.

—Robert Browning

He drew a circle that shut me out — heretic, rebel, a thing to flout.
But love and I had the wit to win — and we drew a circle that took him in!

—Edwin Markham

It is good to have an end to journey toward, but it is the journey that matters in the end.

—Ursula K. LeGuin

I tore myself away from the safe comfort of certainties through my love for truth — and truth rewarded me.

—Simone de Beauvoir

I will not die an unlived life.... I choose to risk my significance; to live so that which comes to me as seed goes to the next as blossom and that which comes to me as blossom, goes on as fruit.

—Dawna Markova

The day will come when, after harnessing space, the winds, the tides and gravitation, we shall harness for God the energies of love. And on that day, for the second time in the history of the world, we shall have discovered fire.

—Pierre Tielhard de Chardin

Some people skate to the puck; I skate to where the puck is going to be.

—Wayne Gretzky

Today is your day! Your mountain is waiting. So, get on your way.

—Dr. Seuss

It's not enough to have a dream,
unless you're willing to pursue it.
It's not enough to know what's right,
unless you're strong enough to do it.
It's not enough to learn the truth,
unless you also learn to live it.
It's not enough to reach for love,
unless you care enough to give it.

—Author Unknown

When you invite trouble, it's usually quick to accept.

—Quoted in *P.S. I Love You*, compiled by H. Jackson Brown, Jr.

Do what you can, with what you have, where you are.

—Theodore Roosevelt

Please be patient. God has not finished with me yet.

—Author Unknown

It is amazing what you can accomplish if you do not care who gets the credit.

—Harry S. Truman

We are not enemies, but friends. We must not be enemies. Though passion may have strained, it must not break our bonds of affection. The mystic cords of memory will swell when again touched as surely they will be by the better angels of our nature.

—Abraham Lincoln

A part of you has grown in me. And so you see, it's you and me together forever and never apart, maybe in distance, but never in heart.

—Author Unknown

Don't walk in front of me, I may not follow. Don't walk behind me, I may not lead. Walk beside me, and just be my friend.

—Albert Camus

If you want to understand democracy, spend less time in the library with Plato, and more time in the buses with people.

—Simeon Strunsky

When the People contend for their liberty, they seldom get anything for their Victory but new Masters.

—George Savile

'Tis known by the name of perseverance in a good cause, and obstinacy in a bad one.

—Laurence Sterne

His voice was as intimate as the rustle of sheets.

—Dorothy Parker

Tact is the art of making a point without making an enemy.

—Howard W. Newton

I find I always have to write something on a steamed mirror.

—Elaine Dundy

Many people's tombstones should read, "Died at 30. Buried at 60."

—Nicholas Murray Butler

No man thoroughly understands a truth until he has contended against it.

—Ralph Waldo Emerson

Virtue is insufficient temptation.

—George Bernard Shaw

The most valuable of all talents is that of never using two words when one will do.

—Thomas Jefferson

Nothing is really work unless you would rather be doing something else.

—James M. Barrie

Most people like hard work. Particularly when they are paying for it.

—Franklin P. Jones

There's a mighty big difference between good, sound reasons and reasons that sound good.

—Burton Hillis

Men will sooner surrender their rights than their customs.

—Moritz Guedemann

If one man offers you democracy and another offers you a bag of grain, at what stage of starvation will you prefer the grain to the vote?

—Bertrand Russell

May you get to Heaven a half hour before the Devil knows you're dead.

—Irish Proverb

We are wide-eyed in contemplating the possibility that life may exist elsewhere in the universe, but we wear blinders when contemplating the possibilities of life on earth.

—Norman Cousins

Man tends to treat all his opinions as principles.

—Herbert Agar

Are you not ashamed of heaping up the greatest amount of money and honour and reputation, and caring so little about wisdom and truth and the greatest improvement of the soul?

—Socrates

Originality is the art of concealing your source.

—Franklin P. Jones

I would rather have men ask why I have no statue than why I have one.

—Marcus Porcius Cato

It is one of the commonest of mistakes to consider that the limit of our power of perception is also the limit of all there is to perceive.

—C.W. Leadbeater

God has no power over the past except to cover it with oblivion.

—Pliny the Elder

And in today already walks tomorrow.

—Samuel Taylor Coleridge

I have seen the future and it is very much like the present — only longer.

—Kehlog Albran

Every nation ridicules other nations, and all are right.

—Arthur Schopenhauer

We know nothing about motivation. All we can do is write books about it.

—Peter Drucker

We would often be ashamed of our finest actions if the world understood all the motives which produced them.

—Duc de La Rochefoucauld

Fame — the aggregate of all the misunderstandings that collect around a new name.

—Rainer Maria Rilke

He that hath wife and children hath given hostages to fortune.

—Francis Bacon

Cooperation is the thorough conviction that nobody can get there unless everybody gets there.

—Virginia Burden, *The Process of Intuition*

Nothing fixes a thing so intensely in the memory as the wish to forget it.

—Michel de Montaigne

Memory is what tells a man that his wife's birthday was yesterday.

—Mario Rocco

The man with a clear conscience probably has a poor memory.

—Author Unknown

I know of no more encouraging fact than the unquestionable ability of man to elevate his life by a conscious endeavor.

—Henry David Thoreau

A man is rich in proportion to the things he can afford to let alone.

—Henry David Thoreau

He gave her a look you could have poured on a waffle.

—Ring Lardner

Hate the sin and love the sinner.

—Mohandas Gandhi

He not only overflowed with learning, but stood in the slop.

—Sydney Smith

The brighter you are, the more you have to learn.

—Don Herold

We see then how far the monuments of wit and learning are more durable than the monuments of power, or of the hands. For have not the verses of Homer continued twenty—five hundred years or more, without the loss of a syllable or letter; during which time infinite palaces, temples, castles, cities have been decayed and demolished?

—Francis Bacon

A little learning is not a dangerous thing to one who does not mistake it for a great deal.

—William Allen White

A society that gives to one class all the opportunities for leisure, and to another all the burdens of work, dooms both classes to spiritual sterility.

—Lewis Mumford

Though I believe in liberalism, I find it difficult to believe in liberals.

—G.K. Chesterton

Liberalism ... is the noblest cry that has ever resounded in this planet.

—José Ortega y Gasset

The course of life is unpredictable ... no one can write his autobiography in advance.

—Abraham Joshua Heschel

One's only real life is the life one never leads.

—Oscar Wilde

The first requisite for immortality is death.

—Stanislaw J. Lec

The tragedy of life is what dies inside a man while he lives.

—Albert Schweitzer

The most important thing in communication is hearing what isn't being said.

—Author Unknown

A weak mind is like a microscope, which magnifies trifling things but cannot receive great ones.

—Lord Chesterfield

But words are things, and a small drop of ink, falling like dew, upon a thought, produces that which makes thousands, perhaps, millions, think.

—Lord Byron, *Don Juan*, 1819

That which we obtain too easily, we esteem too lightly.

—Thomas Paine

Failure to prepare is preparing to fail.

—John Wooden

You can't hold a man down without staying down with him.

—Booker T. Washington

Never tell people how to do things. Tell them what to do and they will surprise you with their ingenuity.

—George S. Patton

If you wish to be brothers, drop your weapons.

—Pope John Paul II

Farming looks mighty easy when your plow is a pencil and you're a thousand miles from the corn field.

—Dwight D. Eisenhower

A writer who wishes to be read by posterity must not be averse to putting hints which might give rise to whole books, or ideas for learned discussions, in some corner of a chapter so that one should think he can afford to throw them away by the thousand.

—George Christoph Lichtenberg

We understand nature by resisting it.

—Gaston Bachelard, *La Formation de l'esprit scientifique*, 1938

I don't think necessity is the mother of invention — invention, in my opinion, arises directly from idleness, possibly also from laziness. To save oneself trouble.

—Agatha Christie, *An Autobiography*, 1977

Novelties *please* less than they *impress*.

—Byron, *Don Juan*, 1824

Order marches with weighty and measured strides; disorder is always in a hurry.

—Napoleon I, *Maxims*, 1815

It is perfectly easy to be original by violating the laws of decency and the canons of good taste.

—Oliver Wendell Holmes, *Over the Teacups*, 1891

Nature has placed man under the government of two sovereign masters, *pain* and *pleasure*.

—Jeremy Bentham, *Principles of Morals and Legislation*, 1789

Without passion man is a mere latent force and possibility, like the flint which awaits the shock of the iron before it can give forth its spark.

—Amiel, *Journal*, 17 December 1856

How poor are they that have not patience!
What wound did ever heal but by degrees?

—William Shakespeare, *Othello*, 1604

I am the fellow citizen of every being that thinks; my country is Truth.

—Alphonse de Lamartine, "*Marseillaise of Peace*," 1841

Experience has taught me this, that we undo ourselves by impatience. Misfortunes have their life and their limits, their sickness and their health.

—Michel de Montaigne

There are many in this old world of ours, who hold that things break about even for all of us. I have observed for example that we all get the same amount of ice. The rich get it in the summertime and the poor get it in the winter.

—Bat Masterson

Calamities are of two kinds: misfortune to ourselves and good fortune to others.

—Ambrose Bierce

The good die young — because they see it's no use living if you've got to be good.

—John Barrymore

It is almost impossible systematically to constitute a natural moral law. Nature has no principles. She furnishes us with no reason to believe that human life is to be respected. Nature, in her indifference, makes no distinction between good and evil.

—Anatole France

Non-cooperation with evil is as much a duty as is cooperation with good.

—Mohandas Gandhi

The only thing necessary for the triumph of evil is for good men to do nothing.

—Edmund Burke

Probably the most honest "self-made man" ever was the one we heard say: "I got to the top the hard way-fighting my own laziness and ignorance every step of the way."

—James Thom

I do not know what I may appear to the world; but to myself I seem to have been only like a boy playing on the sea-shore, and diverting myself in now and then finding a smoother pebble or a prettier shell than ordinary, while the great ocean of truth lay all undiscovered before me.

—Isaac Newton

We do not err because truth is difficult to see. It is visible at a glance. We err because this is more comfortable.

—Alexander Solzhenitsyn

I have never for one instant seen clearly within myself. How then would you have me judge the deeds of others?

—Maurice Maeterlinck

The most powerful weapon on earth is the human soul on fire.

—Ferdinand Foch

The ideals which have lighted my way, and time after time have given me new courage to face life cheerfully, have been kindness, beauty, and truth.

—Albert Einstein, *Ideas and Opinions*

Some people can stay longer in an hour than others can in a week.

—William Dean Howells

More good things in life are lost by indifference than ever were lost by active hostility.

—Robert Gordon Menzies

We can often endure an extra pound of pain far more easily than we can suffer the withdrawal of an ounce of accustomed pleasure.

—Sydney J. Harris

Lots of folks confuse bad management with destiny.

—Kin Hubbard

Opportunity is often difficult to recognize; we usually expect it to beckon us with beepers and billboards.

—William Arthur Ward

Jumping at several small opportunities may get us there more quickly than waiting for one big one to come along.

—Hugh Allen

The most important thing in communication is to hear what isn't being said.

—Peter F. Drucker

An age is called Dark, not because the light fails to shine, but because people refuse to see it.

—James A. Michener, *Space*

Opportunity is a bird that never perches.

—Claude McDonald

Justifying a fault doubles it.

—French Proverb

Most men pursue pleasure with such breathless haste that they hurry past it.

—Soren Kierkegaard

Having someone wonder where you are when you don't come

home at night is a very old human need.

—Margaret Mead

Sometimes the best helping hand you can get is a good, firm push.

—Joann Thomas

In the coldest February, as in every other month in every other year, the best thing to hold on to in this world is each other.

—Linda Ellerbee, *Move On: Adventures in the Real World*

It is often hard to bear the tears that we ourselves have caused.

—Marcel Proust

Children have never been good at listening to their elders, but they have never failed to imitate them.

—James Baldwin

Basically, the only thing we need is a hand that rests on our own, that wishes it well, that sometimes guides us.

—Hector Bianciotti, *Sans La Misericorde du Christ*

There are times when forgetting can be just as important as remembering — and even more difficult.

—Harry and Joan Mier, *Happiness Begins Before Breakfast*

People are living longer than ever before, a phenomenon undoubtedly made necessary by the 30—year mortgage.

—Doug Larson

One sees clearly only with the heart. Anything essential is invisible to the eyes.

—Antoine de Saint—Exupéry, *The Little Prince*, 1943, translated from French by Richard Howard

We all live under the same sky, but we don't have the same horizon.

—Konrad Adenauer

The only person you should ever compete with is yourself. You can't hope for a fairer match.

—Todd Ruthman

Our credulity is greatest concerning the things we know least about. And since we know least about ourselves, we are ready to believe all that is said about us. Hence the mysterious power of both flattery and calumny.

—Eric Hoffer, *The Passionate State of Mind*

Opportunity is as scarce as oxygen; men fairly breathe it and do not know it.

—Doc Sane

Opportunities do not come with their values stamped upon them.

—Maltbie Babcock

Nothing is so often irretrievably missed as a daily opportunity.

—Marie von Ebner—Eschenbach

It is often hard to distinguish between the hard knocks in life and those of opportunity.

—Frederick Phillips

A door that seems to stand open must be a man's size, or it is not the door that Providence means for him.

—Henry Ward Beecher

The eloquent man is he who is no beautiful speaker, but who is inwardly and desperately drunk with a certain belief.

—Ralph Waldo Emerson

To say yes, you have to sweat and roll up your sleeves and plunge both hands into life up to the elbows. It is easy to say no.

—Jean Anouilh

There is no strong performance without a little fanaticism in the performer.

—Ralph Waldo Emerson

The field of consciousness is tiny. It accepts only one problem at a time.

—Antoine de Saint—Exupery

Work and play are words used to describe the same thing under differing conditions.

—Mark Twain

To character and success, two things, contradictory as they may seem, must go together ... humble dependence on God and manly reliance on self.

—William Wordsworth

God's will is not an itinerary, but an attitude.

—Andrew Dhuse

He who would learn to fly one day must first learn to stand and walk and run and climb and dance; one cannot fly into flying.

—Friedrich Nietzsche

Take care of the minutes, for the hours will take care of themselves.

—Lord Chesterfield

Why not learn to enjoy the little things — there are so many of them.

—Author Unknown

Man never made any material as resilient as the human spirit.

—Bern Williams

A problem well stated is a problem half solved.

—Charles F. Kettering

No matter how big and tough a problem may be, get rid of confusion by taking one little step towards solution. Do something. Then try again. At the worst, so long as you don't do it the same way twice, you will eventually use up all the wrong ways of doing it and thus the next try will be the right one.

—George F. Nordenhold

Real difficulties can be overcome, it is only the imaginary ones that are unconquerable.

—Theodore N. Vail

You can overcome anything if you don't bellyache.

—Bernard M. Baruch

I didn't know I'd have to be torn down before I could be built up.

—Author Unknown

Every problem contains within itself the seeds of its own solution.

—Edward Somers

Little things console us because little things afflict us.

—Blaise Pascal

People in distress will sometimes prefer a problem that is familiar to a solution that is not.

—Neil Postman

Untold suffering seldom is.

—Franklin P. Jones

There are three modes of bearing the ills of life: by indifference, by philosophy, and by religion.

—Charles Caleb Colton

The game of life is not so much in holding a good hand as playing a poor hand well.

—H.T. Leslie

Sympathy is never wasted except when you give it to yourself.

—John W. Raper

Self-pity is ... a sinkhole from which no rescuing hand can drag you because you have *chosen* to sink.

—Elizabeth Elliot

Sadness is almost never anything but a form of fatigue.

—Andre Gide

Even the cry from the depths is an affirmation: Why cry if there is no hint of hope of hearing?

—Martin Marty

To exaggerate is to weaken.

—Jean François de La Harpe, *Melanie*, 1770

There are people so addicted to exaggeration they can't tell the truth without lying.

—Josh Billings

Man is inclined to exaggerate almost everything — except his own mistakes.

—Author Unknown

If you're yearning for the good old days, just turn off the air conditioning.

—Griff Niblack

Things ain't what they used to be and probably never was.

—Will Rogers

My mother said to me, "If you become a soldier, you'll be a general, if you become a monk you'll end up as the pope." Instead, I became a painter and wound up as Picasso.

—Pablo Picasso

To travel hopefully is a better thing than to arrive, and the true success is to labor.

—Robert Louis Stevenson, *Virginibus puerisque*, 1881

We should scarcely desire things ardently if we were perfectly acquainted with what we desire.

—Francois de La Rochefoucauld

Granting our wish is one of Fate's saddest jokes.

—James Russell Lowell

Failure and success seem to have been allotted to men by their stars. But they retain the power of wriggling, of fighting with their star or against it, and in the whole universe the only really interesting movement is this wriggle.

—E.M. Forester

If fate means you to lose, give him a good fight anyhow.

—William McFee

Why always "not yet"? Do flowers in spring say "not yet"?

—Norman Douglas

I was seldom able to see an opportunity until it had ceased to be one.

—Mark Twain

Beginnings are apt to be shadowy.

—Rachel Carson

Shun idleness. It is a rust that attaches itself to the most brilliant metals.

—Voltaire

I do not believe in a fate that falls on men however they act; but I do believe in a fate that falls on man unless they act.

—G.K. Chesterton

Seize the opportunity by the beard, for it is bald behind.

—Bulgarian Proverb

If a man would move the world, he must first move himself.

—Socrates

The secret of success in life is for a man to be ready for his opportunity when it comes.

—Benjamin Disraeli

Put your heart, mind, intellect and soul even to your smallest acts. This is the secret of success.

—Swami Sivananda

Many persons wonder why they don't amount to more than they do, have good stuff in them, energetic, persevering, and have ample opportunities. It is all a case of trimming the useless branches and throwing the whole force of power into the development of something that counts.

—Walter J. Johnston

The guts carry the feet, not the feet the guts.

—Miguel de Cervantes

There are at least two kinds of cowards. One kind always lives with himself, afraid to face the world. The other kind lives with the world, afraid to face himself.

—Roscoe Snowden

As a rule, what is out of sight disturbs men's minds more seriously than what they see.

—Julius Caesar

Every difficulty slurred over will be a ghost to disturb your repose later on.

—Frederic Chopin

But friendship is precious, not only in the shade, but in the sunshine of life, and thanks to a benevolent arrangement the greater part of life is sunshine.

—Thomas Jefferson

The soul becomes dyed with the color of its thoughts.

—Marcus Aurelius Antonius

There I am in my younger days, stargazing,
painting picture perfect maps
of how my life and love would be
not counting the unmarked paths of misdirection,
my compass faith in love's perfection
I missed a million miles of road I should have seen.

—Indigo Girls

I shall not let a sorrow die
Until I find the heart of it,
Nor let a wordless joy go by
Until it talks to me a bit.

—Sara Teasdale

If we had keen vision and feeling of all ordinary human life, it would be like hearing the grass grow and the squirrel's heart beat, and we should die of that roar which lies on the other side of silence.

—George Eliot, *Middlemarch*, 1872

A bird does not sing because it has an answer. It sings because it has a song.

—Chinese Proverb

The mind I love must have wild places, a tangled orchard where dark damsons drop in the heavy grass, an overgrown little wood, the chance of a snake or two, a pool that nobody's fathomed the depth of, and paths threaded with flowers planted by the mind.

—Katherine Mansfield

When darkness descends on summer nights, the air around campfires, lanterns and cottage windows becomes filled with swirling moths seemingly intent on self destruction. The suicide fliers are drawn to the flames and light because they normally navigate a straight course by keeping constant the angle of moonlight or sunbeams falling on their eyes. Night lights created by humans disorient moths, causing them to flutter round and round the source without being able to get their bearings.

—Doug Bennet and Tim Tiner, *Up North*

One of the advantages of being disorderly is that one is constantly making exciting discoveries.

—A.A. Milne

Beware a man of one book.

—English Proverb

Like all dreamers, I mistook disenchantment for truth.

—Jean—Paul Sartre

Three passions, simple but overwhelming, have governed my life: the longing for love, the search for knowledge, and unbearable pity for the suffering of mankind.

—Bertrand Russell, *Autobiography*, 1967

Vain the ambition of kings
Who seek by trophies and dead things
To leave a living name behind,
And weave but nets to catch the wind.

—John Webster

It is a mistake to imagine that potentially great men are rare. It is the conditions that permit the promise of greatness to be fulfilled that are rare. What is so difficult to achieve is the cultural background that permits potential greatness to be converted into actual greatness.

—Fred Hoyle, *Of Man and Galaxies*

To be sure of hitting the target, shoot first and, whatever you hit, call it the target.

—Patrick Toche

All that is gold does not glitter,
Not all those who wander are lost.
The old that is strong does not wither,
Deep roots are not reached by the frost.

—J.R.R. Tolkien

A dreamer is one who can only find his way by moonlight, and his punishment is that he sees the dawn before the rest of the world.

—Oscar Wilde

Everything is vague to a degree you do not realize until you have tried to make it precise.

—Bertrand Russell, *The Philosophy of Logical Atomism*

Vision is the art of seeing things invisible.

—Jonathan Swift, "Thoughts on Various Subjects," *Miscellanies*, 1711

Our genes make us immortal.

—*The Secret of Life*, PBS

I wish I could have known earlier that you have all the time you'll need right up to the day you die.

—William Wiley

By daily dying I have come to be.

—Theodore Roethke

Sometimes I've believed as many as six impossible things before breakfast.

—Lewis Carroll

Now, what is it which makes a scene interesting? If you see a man coming through a doorway, it means nothing. If you see him coming through a window — that is at once interesting.

—Billy Wilder

The art of living is the art of knowing how to believe lies.

—Cesare Pavese

All great work is preparing yourself for the accident to happen.

—Sidney Lumet

It is a far, far better thing to have a firm anchor in nonsense than to put out on the troubled seas of thought.

—John Kenneth Galbraith

Anything simple always interests me.

—David Hockney

Training is everything. The peach was once a bitter almond; cauliflower is nothing but cabbage with a college education.

—Mark Twain

Don't try to fix the students, fix ourselves first. The good teacher makes the poor student good and the good student superior. When our students fail, we, as teachers, too, have failed.

—Marva Collins

There are two kinds of people in the world, Notre Dame lovers and Notre Dame haters. And, quite frankly, they're both a pain in the ass.

—Dan Devine, former Notre Dame football coach

The test of a first-rate intelligence is the ability to hold two opposed ideas in the mind at the same time, and still retain the ability to function. One should, for example, be able to see that things are hopeless and yet be determined to make them otherwise.

—F. Scott Fitzgerald

Those who gave away their wings are sad not to see them fly.

—Antonio Porchia

If there were in the world today any large number of people who desired their own happiness more than they desired the unhappiness of others, we could have a paradise in a few years.

—Bertrand Russell

Those who dwell among the beauties and mysteries of the earth are never alone or weary of life.

—Rachel Carson

The block of granite which was an obstacle in the pathway of the weak, became a stepping-stone in the pathway of the strong.

—Thomas Carlyle

Say what you will about the Ten Commandments, you must always come back to the pleasant fact that there are only ten of them.

—H.L. Mencken

Some cause happiness wherever they go; others whenever they go.

—Oscar Wilde

Anybody can win, unless there happens to be a second entry.

—George Ade

The trouble with the world is that the stupid are cocksure and the intelligent are full of doubt.

—Bertrand Russell

The man of virtuous soul commands not, nor obeys.

—Percy Bysshe Shelley, *Queen Mab*

The object of life is not to be on the side of the majority, but to escape finding oneself in the ranks of the insane.

—Marcus Aurelius

We submit to the majority because we have to. But we are not compelled to call our attitude of subjection a posture of respect.

—Ambrose Bierce, *Epigrams*

I see it all perfectly: there are two possibilities, one can either do this or do that. My honest opinion and friendly advice is this: do it or do not do it, you will regret both.

—Kierkegaard

Fear less, hope more; eat less, chew more; whine less, breathe more; hate less, love more; and all good things are yours.

—Swedish Proverb

Let's reintroduce corporal punishment in the schools and use it on the teachers.

—P.J. O'Rourke

A happy childhood is poor preparation for human contacts.

—Colette

I have a wife, I have sons: all of them hostages given to fate.

—Lucan

Many a man has fallen in love with a girl, in a light so dim, he would not have chosen a suit by it.

—Maurice Chevalier

The butterfly counts not months but moments, and has time enough.

—Rabindranath Tagore

I believe in getting into hot water; it keeps you clean.

—G.K. Chesterton

Moderation is a fatal thing; nothing succeeds like excess.

—Oscar Wilde, *A Woman of No Importance*, 1894

Creative minds have always been known to survive any kind of bad training.

—Anna Freud

Happiness is a matter of one's most ordinary and everyday mode of consciousness being busy and lively and unconcerned with self.

—Iris Murdoch

We could have saved the Earth but we were too damned cheap.

—Kurt Vonnegut, Jr.

Only the young die good.

—Oliver Herford

A skeptic is a person who would ask God for his ID card.

—Edgar A. Shoaff

What would there be in a story of happiness? Only what prepares it, only what destroys it can be told.

—André Gide

A man's work is nothing but this slow trek to rediscover, through the detours of art, those two or three great and simple images in whose presence his heart first opened.

—Albert Camus

Yet some things you miss and some things you lose by keeping your arm outstretched.

—Author Unknown

Now all my teachers are dead except silence.

—W.S. Merwin

We are happy when for everything inside us there is a corresponding something outside us.

—W.B. Yeats

Reality is bad enough. Why should I tell the truth?

—Patrick Sky

Unjust. How many times I've used that word, scolded myself with it. All I mean by it now is that I don't have the final courage to say that I refuse to preside over violations against myself, and to hell with justice.

—Lillian Hellman

The most beautiful thing we can experience is the mysterious. It is the source of all true art and science. He to whom the emotion is a stranger, who can no longer pause and stand wrapped in awe, is as good as dead; his eyes are closed.

—Albert Einstein

In nature, there are neither rewards nor punishments; there are consequences.

—Robert Greene Ingersoll, "The New Testament," *Some Reasons Why*, 1881

The Future is something which everyone reaches at the rate of sixty minutes an hour.

—C.S. Lewis

If you haven't all the things you want, be grateful for the things you don't have that you didn't want.

—Author Unknown

If you give what can be taken, you are not really giving. Take what you are given, not what you want to be given. Give what cannot be taken.

—Idries Shah

Individual possession is the great entering wedge, which has split society into eight hundred million fragments.... It virtually, practically, and theoretically denies the brotherhood of man.

—Hiram Stafford, *The Liberator*, 8 September 1844

From the respect paid to property flow, as from a poisoned fountain, most of the evils and vices which render this world such a dreary scene to the contemplative mind.

—Mary Wollstonecroft, *A Vindication of the Rights of Women*

Occident: The part of the world lying west (or east) of the Orient. It is largely inhabited by Christians, a powerful subtribe of the Hypocrites, whose principal industries are murder and cheating, which they are pleased to call "war" and "commerce." These, also, are the principal industries of the Orient.

—Ambrose Bierce, *The Devil's Dictionary*

Having your fate rest in the hands of a jury is the same as entrusting yourself to surgery with a mentally retarded doctor.

—Bill Messing, quoted in *Dream World*, by Fred Woodworth

The terrifying breakdown of social cohesion in the American city, in spite of intense institutionalized police surveillance equipped with every sophisticated aid to public control, illustrates that social behaviour depends upon mutual responsibility rather than upon the policeman.

—Colin Ward, *Anarchy in Action*

America is just the country that shows how all the written guarantees in the world for freedom are no protection against tyranny and oppression of the worst kind. There the politician has come to be looked upon as the very scum of society.

—Peter Kroptkin, speech, 1891

Life, if well lived, is long enough.

—Seneca, *De Ira*

Disobedience, the rarest and most courageous of the virtues, is seldom distinguished from neglect, the laziest and commonest of the vices.

—George Bernard Shaw, *Maxims for Revolutionists*

Thus Dante's motto over Inferno applies with equal force to marriage: "Ye who enter here leave all hope behind."

—Emma Goldman, *Marriage and Love*

If love does not know how to give and take without restrictions, it is not love, but a transaction that never fails to lay stress on a plus and a minus.

—Emma Goldman, *The Tragedy of Women's Emancipation*

A pair of powerful spectacles has sometimes sufficed to cure a person in love.

—Friedrich Nietzsche, *Human, All Too Human*

It used to take me all vacation to grow a new hide in place of the one they flogged off me during school term.

—Mark Twain

History teaches us that men and nations behave wisely once they have exhausted all other alternatives.

—Abba Eban

Education is learning what you didn't know you didn't know.

—George Boas

Education: the inculcation of the incomprehensible into the indifferent by the incompetent.

—John Maynard Keynes

Show me a woman who doesn't feel guilty and I'll show you a man.

—Erica Jong

I can eat a man, but I'm not sure of the fiber content.

—Jenny Eclair

Deliberation is a function of the many; action is the function of one.

—Charles de Gaulle, *War Memoirs*, 1960

Adolescence: A stage between infancy and adultery.

—Ambrose Bierce, *The Devil's Dictionary*, 1911

Early to rise and early to bed
Makes a man healthy and wealthy and dead.

—James Thurber, *Fables for Our Times*, 1940

There is no such thing as pure pleasure; some anxiety always goes with it.

—Ovid, *Metamorphoses*

I love the valiant; but it is not enough to wield a broadsword, one must also know against whom.

—Nietzsche, *Thus Spake Zarathustra*, 1892

All men are rapists and that's all they are. They rape us with their eyes, their laws, and their codes.

—Marilyn French

New Year's Day;
Nothing good or bad, —
Just human beings.

—Shiki

Men are no more immune from emotions than women; we think women are more emotional because the culture lets them give free vent to certain feelings, "feminine" ones, that is, no anger please, but it's okay to turn on the waterworks.

—Una Stannard

An idea that is not dangerous is unworthy to be called an idea at all.

—Elbert Hubbard

Thirty-five is when you finally get your head together and your body starts falling apart.

—Caryn Leschen

The world needs dreamers and the world needs doers. But above all, the world needs dreamers who do.

—Sarah Ban Breathnach, *Simple Abundance: A Daybook of Comfort and Joy*, 1996

The essence of success is that it is never necessary to think of a new idea oneself. It is far better to wait until somebody else does it, and then to copy him in every detail, except his mistakes.

—Aubrey Menen

The ability to reduce everything to simple fundamental laws does not imply the ability to start from those laws and reconstruct the universe.

—Philip W. Anderson, "More Is Different," *Science Magazine*

The weirder you're going to behave, the more normal you should look. It works in reverse, too. When I see a kid with three or four rings in his nose, I know there is absolutely nothing extraordinary about that person.

—P.J. O'Rourke

The church is the great lost and found department.

—Robert Short

The world owes all its onward impulses to men ill at ease. The happy man inevitably confines himself within ancient limits.

—Nathaniel Hawthorne

I slept with faith and found a corpse in my arms on awakening; I drank and danced all night with doubt and found her a virgin in the morning.

—Aleister Crowley, *Book of Lies*

Life's too short for chess.

—Henry James Byron, *Our Boys*, 1874

Perhaps all pleasure is only relief.

—William Burroughs

Isn't it amazing the way the future succeeds in creating an appropriate past?

—John Leonard

Order, unity, and continuity are human inventions, just as truly as catalogues and encyclopedias.

—Bertrand Russell

The formula "two and two make five" is not without its attractions.

—Fyodor Dostoevsky, *Notes from the Underground*, 1864

We all know that Art is not truth. Art is a lie that makes us realize truth, at least the truth that is given us to understand. The artist must know the manner whereby to convince others of the truthfulness of his lies.

—Pablo Picasso

An idea isn't responsible for the people who believe in it.

—Don Marquis

We need not destroy the past. It is gone.

—John Cage

Reason and justice tell me there's more love for humanity in electricity and steam than in chastity and vegetarianism.

—Anton Chekhov

Complete possession is proved only by giving. All you are unable to give possesses you.

—Andre Gide

A mind all logic is like a knife all blade.

—Rabindranath Tagore

Education is what remains after one has forgotten what one has learned in school.

—Albert Einstein

Truth is a great flirt.

—Franz Liszt

Nothing is more conducive to peace of mind than not having any opinion at all.

—G.C. Lichtenberg

One day, someone showed me a glass of water that was half full. And he said, "Is it half full or half empty?" So I drank the water. No more problem.

—Alexander Jodorowsky

If all men are born free, how is it that all women are born slaves?

—Mary Astell

A man never knows how to say goodbye; a woman never knows when to say it.

—Helen Rowland

Whatever our souls are made of, his and mine are the same.

—Emily Brontë

By the time you're his
Shivering and sighing,
And he vows his passion is
Infinite, undying
Lady, make a note of this:
One of you is lying.

—Dorothy Parker

Plain women know more about men than beautiful ones do.

—Katharine Hepburn

After a few years of marriage a man can look right at a woman without seeing her and a woman can see right through a man without looking at him.

—Helen Rowland

The only real progress lies in learning to be wrong all alone.

—Albert Camus

We are asleep with compasses in our hands.

—W.S. Merwin

Perhaps all the dragons of our lives are princesses who are only waiting to see us once beautiful and brave.

—Rainer Maria Rilke

The first step ... shall be to lose the way.

—Galway Kinnell

When Gandhi was asked what he thought of western civilization, he said, "It would be nice."

There's an alternative. There's always a third way, and it's not a combination of the other two ways. It's a different way.

—David Carradine

He liked to go from A to B without inventing letters between.

—John McPhee

The multitude of books is making us ignorant.

—Voltaire

The flood of print has turned reading into a process of gulping rather than savoring.

—Warren Chappell

The faculty of attention has utterly vanished from the Anglo-Saxon mind, extinguished at its source by the big bayadère of journalism, of the newspaper and the picture magazine which keeps screaming, "Look at me." Illustrations, loud simplifications ... bill poster advertising — only these stand a chance.

—Henry James

We often think that when we have completed our study of *one* we know all about *two*, because "two" is "one and one." We forget that we still have to make a study of "and."

—A. Eddington

Life is intrinsically, well, boring and dangerous at the same time. At any given moment the floor may open up. Of course, it almost never does; that's what makes it so boring.

—Edward Gorey

Whatever I take, I take too much or too little; I do not take the exact amount. The exact amount is no use to me.

—Antonio Porchia

Who has not sat before his own heart's curtain? It lifts: and the scenery is falling apart.

—Rainer Maria Rilke

If you think you're free, there's no escape possible.

—Ram Dass

I was right not to be afraid of any thief but myself, who will end by leaving me nothing.

—Katherine Anne Porter

Wandering re-establishes the original harmony which once existed between man and the universe.

—Anatole France

The map is not the territory.

—Alfred Korzybski

There are two kinds of light — the glow that illuminates, and the glare that obscures.

—James Thurber

Everybody gets so much information all day long that they lose their common sense.

—Gertrude Stein

The rose has thorns only for those who would gather it.

—Chinese Proverb

When a woman behaves like a man why doesn't she behave like a nice man?

—Edith Evans

If a thousand old beliefs were ruined in our march to truth we must still march on.

—Stopford Brooke

We swallow greedily any lie that flatters us, but we sip only little by little at a truth we find bitter.

—Denis Diderot

If truth is beauty, how come no one has their hair done in a library.

—Lily Tomlin

Not the power to remember, but its very opposite, the power to forget, is a necessary condition for our existence.

—Sholem Asch, *The Nazarene*, 1939

The most essential gift for a good writer is a built-in, shock-proof, shit detector. This is the writer's radar and all great writers have had it.

—Ernest Hemingway

Not everything that is faced can be changed, but nothing can be changed until it is faced.

—James Baldwin

The people never give up their liberties but under some delusion.

—Edmund Burke

I hold it to be the inalienable right of anybody to go to hell in his own way.

—Robert Frost

Forgive, O Lord, my little jokes on Thee
And I'll forgive Thy great big one on me.

—Robert Frost, "Cluster of Faith," *In the Clearing*, 1962

It's hard for me to get used to these changing times. I can remember when the air was clean and sex was dirty.

—George Burns

One cannot and must not try to erase the past merely because it does not fit the present.

—Golda Meir

I have great faith in fools; self-confidence my friends call it.

—Edgar Allan Poe

The most savage controversies are those about matters as to which there is no good evidence either way. Persecution is used in theology, not in arithmetic.

—Bertrand Russell

For my part I believe in the forgiveness of sin and the redemption of ignorance.

—Adlai Stevenson

He has all the virtues I dislike and none of the vices I admire.

—Winston Churchill

A fanatic is one who can't change his mind and won't change the subject.

—Winston Churchill

Earth gets its price for what Earth gives us;
The beggar is taxed for a corner to die in, ...

—James Russell Lowell, *The Vision of Sir Launfal*, 1848

There are many things which we can afford to forget which it is yet well to learn.

—Oliver Wendell Holmes, Jr.

Bad as I like ye, it's worse without ye.

—Irish Proverb

Men hate to be misunderstood, and to be understood makes them furious.

—Edgar Saltus

The existence of forgetting has never been proved: We only know that some things don't come to mind when we want them.

—Friedrich Nietzsche

It is discouraging to try to penetrate a mind like yours. You ought to get it out and dance on it. That would take some of the rigidity out of it.

—Mark Twain

Loneliness ... is and always has been the central and inevitable experience of every man.

—Thomas Wolfe

If a man in the morning hear the right way, he may die in the evening without regret.

—Confucius

It wasn't until quite late in life that I discovered how easy it is to say "I don't know!"

—Somerset Maugham

Human beings are perhaps never more frightening than when they are convinced beyond doubt that they are right.

—Laurens Van Der Post

If we had no faults of our own, we would not take so much pleasure in noticing those of others.

—Francois duc de la Rochefoucauld

And be these juggling friends no more believ'd,

That palter with us in a double sense;
That keep the word of promise to our ear
And break it to our hope.

—William Shakespeare

We promise according to our hopes, and perform according to our fears.

—Francois duc de la Rochefoucauld

The marvelous rebellion of man at all signs reading "Keep Off."

—Carl Sandburg

I was seized by the stern hand of Compulsion, that dark, unseasonable Urge that impels women to clean house in the middle of the night.

—James Thurber

Without geography, you're nowhere.

—Author Unknown

A criminal becomes a popular figure because he unburdens in no small degree the consciences of his fellow man, for now they know once more where evil is to be found.

—Carl G. Jung

Who depends on another man's table often dines late.

—John Ray

Oft expectation fails, and most oft there
Where most it promises.

—William Shakespeare

It is easier to mend neglect than to quicken love.

—Saint Jerome

In play there are two pleasures for your choosing —
The one is winning, and the other losing.

—Lord Byron

NATURE

Man's heart away from nature becomes hard.

—Standing Bear

How glorious a greeting the sun gives the mountains!

—John Muir

Adopt the pace of nature: her secret is patience.

—Ralph Waldo Emerson

I love to think of nature as an unlimited broadcasting station, through which God speaks to us every hour, if we will only tune in.

—George Washington Carver

How strange that Nature does not knock, and yet does not intrude!

—Emily Dickinson, letter to Mrs. J.S. Cooper, 1880

I only went out for a walk and finally concluded to stay out till sundown, for going out, I found, was really going in.

—John Muir, 1913, in L.M. Wolfe, ed., *John Muir, John of the Mountains: The Unpublished Journals of John Muir*, 1938

Look at the trees, look at the birds, look at the clouds, look at the stars ... and if you have eyes you will be able to see that the whole existence is joyful. Everything is simply happy. Trees are happy for no reason; they are not going to become prime ministers or presidents and they are not going to become rich and they will never have any bank balance. Look at the flowers — for no reason. It is simply unbelievable how happy flowers are.

—Osho

Climb the mountains and get their good tidings. Nature's peace will flow into you as sunshine flows into trees. The winds will blow their own freshness into you, and the storms their energy, while cares will drop off like autumn leaves.

—John Muir

Forget not that the earth delights to feel your bare feet and the winds long to play with your hair.

—Kahlil Gibran

I think it pisses God off if you walk by the color purple in a field somewhere and don't take notice.

—Alice Walker, *The Color Purple*, 1982

I am not bound for any public place, but for ground of my own where I have planted vines and orchard trees, and in the heat of the day climbed up into the healing shadow of the woods. Better than any argument is to rise at dawn and pick dew—wet red berries in a cup.

—Wendell Berry

And how should a beautiful, ignorant stream of water know it heads for an early release — out across the desert, running toward the Gulf, below sea level, to murmur its lullaby, and see the Imperial Valley rise out of burning sand with cotton blossoms, wheat, watermelons, roses, how should it know?

—Carl Sandburg, *Good Morning America*, 1928

I thank you God for this most amazing day, for the leaping greenly spirits of trees, and for the blue dream of sky and for everything which is natural, which is infinite, which is yes.

—E.E. cummings

The poetry of the earth is never dead.

—John Keats

I remember a hundred lovely lakes, and recall the fragrant breath of pine and fir and cedar and poplar trees. The trail has strung upon it, as upon a thread of silk, opalescent dawns and saffron sunsets. It has given me blessed release from care and worry and the troubled thinking of our modern day. It has been a return to the primitive and the peaceful. Whenever the pressure of our complex city life thins my blood and benumbs my brain, I seek relief in the trail; and when I hear the coyote wailing to the yellow dawn, my cares fall from me — I am happy.

—Hamlin Garland, *McClure's*, February 1899

In wilderness I sense the miracle of life, and behind it our scientific accomplishments fade to trivia.

—Charles A. Lindbergh, *Life*, 22 December 1967

After all, I don't see why I am always asking for private, individual, selfish miracles when every year there are miracles like white dogwood.

—Anne Morrow Lindbergh

Never does nature say one thing and wisdom another.

—Juvenal, *Satires*

There is a pleasure in the pathless woods,
There is a rapture on the lonely shore,
There is society, where none intrudes,
By the deep sea, and music in its roar:
I love not man the less, but Nature more.

—George Gordon, Lord Byron, *Childe Harold's Pilgrimage*, 1818

You can't be suspicious of a tree, or accuse a bird or a squirrel of subversion or challenge the ideology of a violet.

—Hal Borland, *Sundial of the Seasons*, 1964

The sun, with all those planets revolving around it and dependent on it, can still ripen a bunch of grapes as if it had nothing else in the universe to do.

—Galileo

I believe a leaf of grass is no less than the journey-work of the stars.

—Walt Whitman

Some keep the Sabbath going to Church,
I keep it staying at Home —
With a bobolink for a Chorister,
And an Orchard, for a Dome.

—Emily Dickinson

To sit in the shade on a fine day and look upon verdure is the most perfect refreshment.

—Jane Austen

Good heavens, of what uncostly material is our earthly happiness composed ... if we only knew it. What incomes have we not had from a flower, and how unfailing are the dividends of the seasons.

—James Russell Lowell

Nature does not hurry, yet everything is accomplished.

—Lao Tzu

The sky is the daily bread of the eyes.

—Ralph Waldo Emerson

As you sit on the hillside, or lie prone under the trees of the forest, or sprawl wet-legged by a mountain stream, the great door, that does not look like a door, opens.

—Stephen Graham, *The Gentle Art of Tramping*

Great things are done when men and mountains meet. This is not done by jostling in the street.

—William Blake

To me a lush carpet of pine needles or spongy grass is more welcome than the most luxurious Persian rug.

—Helen Keller

Shall I not have intelligence with the earth? Am I not partly leaves and vegetable mould myself.

—Henry David Thoreau

One touch of nature makes the whole world kin.

—William Shakespeare

To one who has been long in city pent,
'Tis very sweet to look into the fair
And open face of heaven, — to breathe a prayer
Full in the smile of the blue firmament.

—John Keats, *Sonnet XIV*

Fieldes have eies and woods have eares.

—John Heywood, 1565

You must not know too much or be too precise or scientific about birds and trees and flowers and watercraft; a certain free—margin, and even vagueness — ignorance, credulity — helps your enjoyment of these things.

—Henry David Thoreau

A sensitive plant in a garden grew,
And the young winds fed it with silver dew,
And it opened its fan—like leaves to the light,
and closed them beneath the kisses of night.

—Percy Bysshe Shelley, "The Sensitive Plant," 1820

In June as many as a dozen species may burst their buds on a single day. No man can heed all of these anniversaries; no man can ignore all of them.

—Aldo Leopold

Nature hates calculators.

—Ralph Waldo Emerson

Look deep into nature, and then you will understand everything better.

—Albert Einstein

The woods were made for the hunters of dreams,
The brooks for the fishers of song;
To the hunters who hunt for the gunless game
The streams and the woods belong.

—Sam Walter Foss

I've always regarded nature as the clothing of God.

—Alan Hovhaness

Nature reserves the right to inflict upon her children the most terrifying jests.

—Thornton Wilder

And this, our life, exempt from public haunt, finds tongues in trees, books in the running brooks, sermons in stones, and good in everything.

—William Shakespeare

My heart that was rapt away by the wild cherry blossoms — will it return to my body when they scatter?

—Kotomichi

The tulip and the butterfly
Appear in gayer coats than I:
Let me be dressed fine as I will,
Flies, worms, and flowers exceed me still.

—Isaac Watts

I never had any other desire so strong, and so like covetousness, as that.... I might be master at last of a small house and a large garden, with very moderate conveniences joined to them, and there dedicate the remainder of my life to the culture of them and the study of nature.

—Abraham Cowley

Climb up on some hill at sunrise. Everybody needs perspective once in a while, and you'll find it there.

—Robb Sagendorph

What would the world be, once bereft
Of wet and wildness? Let them be left,
O let them be left, wildness and wet,
Long live the weeds and the wildness yet.

—Gerard Manley Hopkins, *Inversnaid*

That we find a crystal or a poppy beautiful means that we are less alone, that we are more deeply inserted into existence than the course of a single life would lead us to believe.

—John Berger, *The Sense of Sight*, 1980

Nature is man's teacher. She unfolds her treasures to his search, unseals his eye, illumes his mind, and purifies his heart; an influence breathes from all the sights and sounds of her existence.

—Alfred Billings Street

There is nothing in the world more peaceful than apple-leaves with an early moon.

—Alice Meynell

Some people worry that artificial intelligence will make us feel inferior, but then, anybody in his right mind should have an inferiority complex every time he looks at a flower.

—Alan C. Kay

Let us permit nature to have her way. She understands her business better than we do.

—Michel de Montaigne

A lawn is nature under totalitarian rule.

—Michael Pollan, *Second Nature*, 1991

I am not a lover of lawns. Rather would I see daisies in their thousands, ground ivy, hawkweed, and even the hated plantain with tall stems, and dandelions with splendid flowers and fairy down, than the too-well-tended lawn.

—W.H. Hudson, *The Book of a Naturalist*, 1919

I go to nature to be soothed and healed, and to have my senses put in order.

—John Burroughs

Any man that walks the mead
In bud, or blade, or bloom, may find
A meaning suited to his mind.

—Alfred Tennyson

Nature will bear the closest inspection. She invites us to lay our eye level with her smallest leaf, and take an insect view of its plain.

—Henry David Thoreau

Nothing is more beautiful than the loveliness of the woods before sunrise.

—George Washington Carver

Breathless, we flung us on a windy hill,

Laughed in the sun, and kissed the lovely grass.

—Rupert Brooke

How cunningly nature hides every wrinkle of her inconceivable antiquity under roses and violets and morning dew!

—Ralph Waldo Emerson

The world is mud—luscious and puddle—wonderful.

—E.E. cummings

Nature chose for a tool, not the earthquake or lightning to rend and split asunder, not the stormy torrent or eroding rain, but the tender snow—flowers noiselessly falling through unnumbered centuries.

—John Muir

Nature, to be commanded, must be obeyed.

—Francis Bacon, *Novum Organum*, 1620

Nature cannot be tricked or cheated. She will give up to you the object of your struggles only after you have paid her price.

—Napoleon Hill

In some mysterious way woods have never seemed to me to be static things. In physical terms, I move through them; yet in metaphysical ones, they seem to move through me.

—John Fowles

I've made an odd discovery. Every time I talk to a savant I feel quite sure that happiness is no longer a possibility. Yet when I talk with my gardener, I'm convinced of the opposite.

—Bertrand Russell

Truly it may be said that the outside of a mountain is good for the inside of a man.

—George Wherry, *Alpine Notes and the Climbing Foot*, 1896

Nature is full of genius, full of the divinity; so that not a snowflake escapes its fashioning hand.

—Henry David Thoreau, *Journal*, 5 January 1856

The mind, in proportion as it is cut off from free communication with nature, with revelation, with God, with itself, loses its life, just as the body droops when debarred from the air and the cheering light from heaven.

—William Channing

Once you have heard the lark, known the swish of feet through hill—top grass and smelt the earth made ready for the seed, you are never again going to be fully happy about the cities and towns that man carries like a crippling weight upon his back.

—Gwyn Thomas

If one way be better than another, that you may be sure is Nature's way.

—Aristotle, *Nichomachean Ethics*

A wee child toddling in a wonder world.... I prefer to their dogma my excursions into the natural gardens where the voice of the Great Spirit is heard in the twittering of birds, the rippling of mighty waters, and the sweet breathing of flowers. If this is Paganism, then at present, at least, I am a Pagan.

—Zitkala—Sa

One impulse from a vernal wood
May teach you more of man,
Of moral evil and of good,
Than all the sages can.

—William Wordsworth, "*The Tables Turned*," 1798

You will find something more in woods than in books. Trees and stones will teach you that which you can never learn from masters.

—St. Bernard

And this our life, exempt from public haunt,
Finds tongues in trees, books in the running brooks,
Sermons in stones, and good in everything.

—William Shakespeare, *As You Like It*, 1599

Nature teaches more than she preaches. There are no sermons in stones. It is easier to get a spark out of a stone than a moral.

—John Burroughs

Nature is the art of God.

—Thomas Browne, *Religio Medici*, 1635

The color of the mountains is Buddha's body; the sound of running water is his great speech.

—Dogen

Earth's crammed with heaven,
And every common bush afire with God;

—Elizabeth Barrett Browning

There is not a sprig of grass that shoots uninteresting to me.

—Thomas Jefferson

Maybe nature is fundamentally ugly, chaotic and complicated. But if it's like that, then I want out.

—Steven Weinberg

To find the universal elements enough; to find the air and the water exhilarating; to be refreshed by a morning walk or an evening saunter; to be thrilled by the stars at night; to be elated over a bird's nest or a wildflower in spring — these are some of the rewards of the simple life.

—John Burroughs

OPPORTUNITY

O, once in each man's life, at least,
Good luck knocks at his door;
And wit to seize the witting guest
Need never hunger more.

—L. J. Bates, *Good Luck*

With doubt and dismay you are smitten,
You think there's no chance for you, son?
Why the best books haven't been written,
The best race hasn't been run.

—Berton Braley, *Opportunity*

Man's extremity is God's opportunity.

—John Flavel. Pamphlet, c. I680

Master of human destinies am I!
Fame, love, and fortune on my footsteps wait.
Cities and fields I walk; I penetrate
Deserts and seas remote, and passing by
Hovel and mart and palace, soon or late
I knock unbidden once at every gate, ...

—J.j. Ingalls, *Opportunity*

They do me wrong who say I come no more
When once I knock and fail to find you in;
For every day I stand outside your door
And bid you wake, and rise to fight and win,

—Walter Malone, *Opportunity*

He that will not when he may,
He shall not when he will,
—Robert Mannyng, *Handlyng Synne* (1303)

There is a tide in the affairs of men,
Which, taken at the flood, leads on to fortune.
—Shakespeare, *Julius Caesar, IV. 3*

OPTIMISM AND PESSIMISM

God's in his Heaven—
All's right with the worldl
—R. Browning, *Pippa Passes*

One who never turned his back but marched breast forward,
Never doubted clouds would break,
Never dreamed, though right were worsted, wrong would triumph,
Held we fall to rise, are baffled to fight better,Sleep to wake.
—R. Browning, *Asolando, Epilogue*

He who, from zone to zone,
Guides through the boundless sky thy certain flight,
In the long way that I must tread alone,
Will lead my steps aright.
—William C. Bryant, To *a Waterfowl*

The place where optimism most flourishes is the lunatic asylum.
—Havelock Ellis, *The Dance of Life*

A health unto the happy,
A fig for him who frets!
It is not raining rain to me,
It's raining violets,
—R. Loveman, *April Rain*

There's a good time coming, boys!
A good time coming,

—Charles Mackay, *The Good Time Coming*

Who brought me hither
Will bring me hence; no other guide I seek,

—Milton, *Paradise Regained, I*

And spite of Pride, in erring Reason's spite,
One truth is clear, *Whatever is, is right.*

—Pope, *Essay on Man, I*

Behold, we know not anything;
I can but trust that good shall fall
At last—far off—at last, to all,

And every winter change to spring,

—Tennyson, *In Memoriam. LIV*

All is for the best in the best of possible worlds,
(Tout est pour le mieux daps le meilleur des mondes pos sibles,)

—Voltaire, *Candide*

I hate the Pollyanna pest
Who says that All is for the Best.

—Franklin P. Adams, *Thoughts on the Cosmos*

The optimist proclaims that we live in the best of all possible worlds; and the pessimist fears this is true.

—Branch Cabell, *The Silver Stallion*

Two men look out through the same bars:
One sees the mud, and one the stars.

—F. Langbridge, A *Cluster of Quiet Thoughts*

Twixt optimist and pessimis'
The difference is droll:
The optimist sees the doughnut,
The pessimist, the hole.
—Mcl. Wilson, *Optimist and Pessimist*

The average pencil is seven inches long, with just a half—inch eraser —in case you thought optimism was dead.
—Robert Brault

Both optimists and pessimists contribute to our society. The optimist invents the airplane and the pessimist the parachute.
—Gil Stern

A pessimist is a man who has been compelled to live with an optimist.
—Elbert Hubbard, *The Note-Book*, 1927

The nice part about being a pessimist is that you are constantly being either proven right or pleasantly surprised.
—George F. Will, *The Leveling Wind*

A pessimist sees only the dark side of the clouds, and mopes; a philosopher sees both sides, and shrugs; an optimist doesn't see the clouds at all — he's walking on them.
—Leonard Louis Levinson

An optimist stays up until midnight to see the new year in. A pessimist stays up to make sure the old year leaves.
—Bill Vaughan

An optimist is the human personification of spring.
—Susan J. Bissonette

An optimist is a person who starts a new diet on Thanksgiving Day.
—Irv Kupcinet

Being an optimist after you've got everything you want doesn't count.

—Kin Hubbard

Optimists are nostalgic about the future.

—Chicago Tribune

Optimism is the foundation of courage.

—Nicholas Murray Butler

A pessimist is one who makes difficulties of his opportunities and an optimist is one who makes opportunities of his difficulties.

—Harry Truman

Some people are so fond of ill-luck that they run half-way to meet it.

—Douglas Jerrold, "*Meeting Troubles Half—Way*," 1859

In the long run the pessimist may be proved right, but the optimist has a better time on the trip.

—Daniel L. Reardon

It doesn't hurt to be optimistic. You can always cry later.

—Lucimar Santos de Lima

Optimism is a kind of heart stimulant — the digitalis of failure.

—Elbert Hubbard

An optimist is merely an ex—pessimist with his pockets full of money, his digestion in good condition, and his wife in the country.

—Helen Rowland

Pessimist: One who, when he has the choice of two evils, chooses both.

—Oscar Wilde

A pessimist is a man who thinks all women are bad. An optimist is a man who hopes they are.

—Chauncey Mitchell Depew

There is no sadder sight than a young pessimist.

—Mark Twain

The basis of optimism is sheer terror.

—Oscar Wilde

How many pessimists end up by desiring the things they fear, in order to prove that they are right?

—Robert Mallett, *Apostilles*, 1972

An optimist is a guy
that has never had
much experience.

—Don Marquis, *archy and mehitabel*, 1927

Always borrow money from a pessimist, he doesn't expect to be paid back.

—Author Unknown

PASSION

It is with our passions, as it is with fire and water, they are good servants but bad masters,

—Sir Roger Uestrange, *Aesop, 38*

On life's vast ocean diversely we sail.
Reason the card, but Passion is the gale.

—Pope, *Moral Essays, I*

Give me that man
That is not passion's slave, and I will wear him
In my heart's core, ay, in my heart of heart.

—Shakespeare, *Hamlet, III, 2*

PEACE

I prefer the most unjust peace to the justest war that was ever waged.

—Cicero, *Letters to Atticus*

In His will is our peace,
(In *la sua coluntade e nostra pace.)*

—Dante, *Paradise*, Ill

Peace with honor.

—B. Disraeli, Speech, I878

Let us have peace.

—U. S. Grant, Letter, 1868

Peace at any price,

—Lamartine (as quoted by A. H, Clough)

Buried was the bloody hatchet;
Buried was the dreadful war club;
Buried were all warlike weapons,
And the war cry was forgotten.
There was peace among the nations.

—Longfellow, *Hiawatha, X111*

War in men's eyes shall be
A monster of iniquity
In the good time corning.
Nations shall not quarrel then,
To prove which is the stronger;
Nor slaughter men for glory's sake;—
Wait a little longer.

—C. Mackay, The Good Time Coming

In proportion as the antagonism between the classes vanishes, the hostility of the nation to another will come to an end.

—Marx And Engels, *Communist Manifesto*

Peace hath her victories
No less renown'd than war,

—Milton. *Sonnet: To the Lord Gen. Cromwell*

Blessed are the peace-makers.

—New Testament, *Matthew, V, 9*

Glory to God in the highest, and peace on earth, good will toward men.

—New Testament, *Luke, IT, I4*

The peace of God which passeth all understanding.

—New Testament, *Philippians, IV, 7*

How beautiful upon the mountains are the feet of him that bringeth good tidings, that publisheth peace.

—Old Testament, *Isaiah, L11, 7*

Peace, peace; where there is no peace.

—Old Testament, *Jeremiah, VI, I4*

The wolf also shall dwell with the lamb, and the leopard shall lie down with the kid.

—Old Testament, *Isaiah, XI, 6*

They shall beat their swords into ploughshares, and their spears into pruning hooks: nation shall not lift sword against nation, neither shall they learn war any more.

—Old Testament, *Isaiah, II, 4*

Till the war—drum cnrobb'd no longer and the battle—flags were

furi'd
In the Parliament of man, the Federation of the world.

—Tennyson, *Locksley Hall*

Why do they prate of the blessings of peace? we have made them a curse, …
And lust of gain, in the spirit of Cain, is it better or worse Than the heart of the citizen hissing in war.…

—Tennyson, *Maud, I*

They have not wanted *Peace* at all; they have wanted to be spared war—as though the absence of war was the same as peace.

—Dorothy Thompson, On *the Record*

It must be a peace without victory.

—Woodrow wilson, Address to Senate, Jan., 1917

God for His service needeth not proud work of human skill;
They please Him best who labour most in peace to do His Will,

—Wordsworth, *The Poet's Dream*

Let there be peace on earth
And let it begin with me.

—Seymour Miller & Jill Jackson, "Let There Be Peace on Earth," 1955

I take it that what all men are really after is some form of, perhaps only some formula of, peace.

—James Conrad

The real differences around the world today are not between Jews and Arabs; Protestants and Catholics; Muslims, Croats, and Serbs. The real differences are between those who embrace peace and those who would destroy it; between those who look to the future and those who cling to the past; between those who open their arms and those who are determined to clench their fists.

—William J. Clinton, 1997

We look forward to the time when the Power of Love will replace the Love of Power. Then will our world know the blessings of peace.

—William Ewart Gladstone

If we have no peace, it is because we have forgotten that we belong to each other.

—Mother Teresa

Peace cannot be achieved through violence, it can only be attained through understanding.

—Ralph Waldo Emerson

If they want peace, nations should avoid the pin-pricks that precede cannon shots.

—Napoleon Bonaparte

The more we sweat in peace the less we bleed in war.

—Vijaya Lakshmi Pandit

The pacifist's task today is to find a method of helping and healing which provides a revolutionary constructive substitute for war.

—Vera Brittain, 1964

You cannot shake hands with a clenched fist.

—Golda Meir

Peace hath higher tests of manhood

Than battle ever knew.

—John Greenleaf Whittier

Five great enemies to peace inhabit with us: avarice, ambition, envy, anger, and pride. If those enemies were to be banished, we should infallibly enjoy perpetual peace.

—Francesco Petrarch

Yes, we love peace, but we are not willing to take wounds for it, as we are for war.

—John Andrew Holmes, *Wisdom in Small Doses*

An eye for eye only ends up making the whole world blind.

—Mahatma Gandhi

There is one armor that the world of men and women, as a world, has never yet put on. The churches have long bungled with its fastenings, but the world has gone unfended, and few have been those in whose hands the mystical sword of the spirit has shone with daily use. This armor, waiting to be worn, is the armor of brotherhood and sacrifice, the world of unselfishness, a conquering sword, with the power, where used, to unite the world in love. And there are none who may not put it on.

—M.A. DeWolfe Howe

I think that people want peace so much that one of these days government had better get out of their way and let them have it.

—Dwight Eisenhower

Lord, bid war's trumpet cease;
Fold the whole earth in peace.

—Oliver Wendell Holmes

We have all taken risks in the making of war. Isn't it time that we should take risks to secure peace?

—J. Ramsay MacDonald

We seek peace, knowing that peace is the climate of freedom.

—Dwight D. Eisenhower

A warless world will come as men develop warless hearts.

—Charles Wesley Burns

We shall never be able to effect physical disarmament until we have succeeded in effecting moral disarmament.

—J. Ramsay MacDonald

Right is more precious than peace.

—Woodrow Wilson

Maybe we should develop a Crayola bomb as our next secret weapon. A happiness weapon. A beauty bomb. And every time a crisis developed, we would launch one. It would explode high in the air — explode softly — and send thousands, millions, of little parachutes into the air. Floating down to earth — boxes of Crayolas. And we wouldn't go cheap, either — not little boxes of eight. Boxes of sixty-four, with the sharpener built right in. With silver and gold and copper, magenta and peach and lime, amber and umber and all the rest. And people would smile and get a little funny look on their faces and cover the world with imagination.

—Robert Fulghum

In the name of peace
They waged the wars
Ain't they got no shame

—Nikki Giovanni

PHILOSOPHY

Philosophy is nothing but common sense in a dress suit.

—Author Unknown

Get married, in any case. If you happen to get a good mate, you will be happy; if a bad one, you will become philosophical, which is a fine thing in itself.

—Socrates, in Diogenes Laertius, *Lives*

When he to whom one speaks does not understand, and he who speaks himself does not understand, that is metaphysics.

—Voltaire, *Philosophical Dictionary*

We live in a world in which politics has replaced philosophy.

—Martin L. Gross, *A Call for Revolution*, 1993

When I study philosophical works I feel I am swallowing something which I don't have in my mouth.

—Albert Einstein

The point of philosophy is to start with something so simple as not to seem worth stating, and to end with something so paradoxical that no one will believe it.

—Bertrand Russell

Leisure is the Mother of Philosophy.

—Thomas Hobbes

The only difference between graffiti and philosophy is the word "fuck."

—Author Unknown

Philosophy is just a hobby. You can't open a philosophy factory.

—Dewey Selmon

God offers to every mind its choice between truth and repose. Take which you please — you can never have both.

—Ralph Waldo Emerson

My definition [of a philosopher] is of a man up in a balloon, with his family and friends holding the ropes which confine him to earth and trying to haul him down.

—Louisa May Alcott, in *Life, Letters, and Journals*, ed. E.D. Cheney, 1889

Philosophy begins in wonder. And, at the end, when philosophic thought has done its best, the wonder remains.

—Alfred North Whitehead

If everybody contemplates the infinite instead of fixing the drains, many of us will die of cholera.

—John Rich

Upon the whole, I am inclined to think that the far greater part, if not all, of those difficulties which have hitherto amused philosophers, and blocked up the way to knowledge, are entirely owing to our selves. That we have first raised a dust, and then complain, we cannot see.

—George Berkeley

To live alone one must be a beast or a god, says Aristotle. Leaving out the third case: one must be both — a philosopher.

—Friedrich Nietzsche

Being a philosopher, I have a problem for every solution.

—Robert Zend

Metaphysics is a dark ocean without shores or lighthouse, strewn with many a philosophic wreck.

—Immanuel Kant

Nobody can have the consolations of religion or philosophy unless he has first experienced their desolations.

—Aldous Huxley, *Themes and Variations*, 1950

Philosophers, for the most part, are constitutionally timid, and dislike the unexpected. Few of them would be genuinely happy as pirates or burglars. Accordingly they invent systems which make the future calculable, at least in its main outlines.

—Bertrand Russell

To teach how to live with uncertainty, yet without being paralyzed by hesitation, is perhaps the chief thing that philosophy can do.

—Bertrand Russell

If you've never met a student from the University of Chicago, I'll describe him to you. If you give him a glass of water, he says, "This is a glass of water. But is it a glass of water? And if it is a glass of water, why is it a glass of water?" And eventually he dies of thirst.

—Shelley Berman

What is the first business of philosophy? To part with self—conceit. For it is impossible for anyone to begin to learn what he thinks that he already knows.

—Epictetus, *Discourses*

Philosophy is a state of fermentation, a process without final outcome.

—Esa Saarinen

To ridicule philosophy is really to philosophize.

—Blaise Pascal, *Pensées*, 1670

We come late, if at all, to wine and philosophy: whiskey and action are easier.

—Mignon McLaughlin, *The Neurotic's Notebook*, 1960

Philosophy will clip an angel's wings,
Conquer all mysteries by rule and line,
Empty the haunted air, and gnomed mine —Unweave a rainbow.

—John Keats, "*Lamia*," 1819

Religion is a man using a divining rod. Philosophy is a man using a pick and shovel.

—Author Unknown

I was thrown out of college for cheating on the metaphysics exam: I looked into the soul of another boy.

—Woody Allen

I also realized that the philosophers, far from ridding me of my vain doubts, only multiplied the doubts that tormented me and failed to remove any one of them. So I chose another guide and said, Let me follow the Inner Light; it will not lead me so far astray as others have done, or if it does it will be my own fault, and I shall not go so far wrong if I follow my own illusions as if I trusted to their deceits.

—Jean Jacques Rousseau

Learning Zen is a phenomenon of gold and dung. Before you understand it, it's like gold; after you understand it, it's like dung.

—Zen Saying

Philosophy triumphs easily over past evils and future evils; but present evils triumph over it.

—La Rochefoucauld, *Maxims*, 1678

Philosophy: A route of many roads leading from nowhere to nothing.

—Ambrose Bierce, *The Enlarged Devil's Dictionary*

It's easy 'nough to titter w'en de stew is smokin' hot,
But hit's mighty ha'd to giggle w'en dey's nuffin' in de pot,

—Paul Laurence Dunbar, *Philosophy*

Philosophy is the highest music.

—Plato, *Phaedo*

It is a great advantage for a system of philosophy to be substantially true.

—Santayana, *The Unknowable*

For there was never yet philosopher
That could endure the toothache patiently,

—Shakespeare, *Much Ado About Nothing, V, 1*

There are more things in heaven and earth, Horatio,
They are dreamt of in your philosophy.

—Shakespeare, *Hamlei, I, 5*

PLANET EARTH

Give me matter and I will construct a world out of it!

—Immanuel Kant

The world is large,
when its weary leagues two loving hearts divide;
But the world is small,

when your enemy is loose on the other side.

—John Boyle O'reilly

We have it in our power to begin the world over again.

—Thomas Paine

The world of the future will not flourish behind walls—no matter who builds them and no matter what their purpose. A world divided economically must inevitably be a world divided politically. As Secretary of State, I cannot contemplate that prospect with anything but deep disquiet.

—William P. Rogers

Physicists and astronomers see their own implications in the world being round, but to me it means that only one-third of the world is asleep at any given time and the other two-thirds is up to something.

—Dean Rusk

POWER

Our real problem, then, is not our strength today; it is rather the vital necessity of action today to ensure our strength tomorrow.

—Dwight D. Eisenhower

We all have enough strength to endure the misfortunes of others.

—François De La Rochefoucauld

It is from weakness that people reach for dictators and concentrated government power. Only the strong can be free. And only the productive can be strong.

—Wendell Willkie

REFORMATION

A reyformer thinks he was ilicted because he was a reyformer, whin th' thruth iv th' matther is he was ilicted because no wan knew him.

—Finley Peter Dunne

The voice of great events is proclaiming to us, reform, that you may preserve.

—Thomas Babington Macaulay

The best reformers the world has ever seen are those who commence on themselves.

—Attributer to George Bernard Shaw

REMEDY

There is always an easy solution to every human problem—neat, plausible and wrong.

—H. L. Mencken

RESPONSIBILITY

If you want children to keep their feet on the ground, put some responsibility on their shoulders.

—Abigail Van Buren

"I must do something" always solves more problems than "Something must be done."

—Author Unknown

"It's a question of discipline," the little prince told me later on. "When you've finished washing and dressing each morning, you must tend your planet."

—Antoine de Saint—Exupéry, *The Little Prince*, 1943, translated from French by Richard Howard

Responsibility: A detachable burden easily shifted to the shoulders of God, Fate, Fortune, Luck or one's neighbor. In the days of astrology it was customary to unload it upon a star.

—Ambrose Bierce, *The Devil's Dictionary*, 1911

Ef you take a sword an' dror it,
An' go stick a feller thru,
Guv'ment ain't to answer for it,
God'll send the bill to you.

—James Russell Lowell

Responsibility's like a string we can only see the middle of. Both ends are out of sight.

—William McFee, *Casuals of the Sea*, 1916

The willingness to accept responsibility for one's own life is the source from which self—respect springs.

—Joan Didion

Most of us can read the writing on the wall; we just assume it's addressed to someone else.

—Ivern Ball

The great thought, the great concern, the great anxiety of men is to restrict, as much as possible, the limits of their own responsibility.

—Giosué Borsi

We need to restore the full meaning of that old word, duty. It is the other side of rights.

—Pearl Buck

Why do children want to grow up? Because they experience their lives as constrained by immaturity and perceive adulthood as a condition of greater freedom and opportunity. But what is there today, in America, that very poor and very rich adolescents want to do but cannot do? Not much: they can "do" drugs, "have" sex, "make" babies, and "get" money (from their parents, crime, or the State). For such adolescents, adulthood becomes synonymous with responsibility rather than liberty. Is it any surprise that they remain adolescents?

—Thomas Szasz

With every civil right there has to be a corresponding civil obligation.

—Edison Haines

I believe that every right implies a responsibility; every opportunity, an obligation; every possession, a duty.

—John D. Rockefeller Jr.

We have the Bill of Rights. What we need is a Bill of Responsibilities.

—Bill Maher

Take your life in your own hands, and what happens? A terrible thing: no one to blame.

—Erica Jong

When you blame others, you give up your power to change.

—Author Unknown

Even when we know what is right, too often we fail to act. More often we grab greedily for the day, letting tomorrow bring what it will, putting off the unpleasant and unpopular.

—Bernard M. Baruch

Duty is what one expects from others.

—Oscar Wilde

A new position of responsibility will usually show a man to be a far stronger creature than was supposed.

—William James

Mistakes fail in their mission of helping the person who blames them on the other fellow.

—Henry S. Haskins

Few things help an individual more than to place responsibility upon him, and to let him know that you trust him.

—Booker T. Washington

God has entrusted me with myself.

—Epictetus

We have not passed that subtle line between childhood and adulthood until ... we have stopped saying "It got lost," and say "I lost it."

—Sidney J. Harris

It is easy to ignore responsibility when one is only an intermediate link in a chain of action.

—Stanley Milgram

When a man points a finger at someone else, he should remember that four of his fingers are pointing at himself.

—Louis Nizer

Whether or not you have children yourself, you are a parent to the next generation. If we can only stop thinking of children as individual property and think of them as the next generation, then we can realize we all have a role to play.

—Charlotte Davis Kasl, *Finding Joy*, 1994

Action springs not from thought, but from a readiness for responsibility.

—Dietrich Bonhoeffer

The commands of democracy are as imperative as its privileges and opportunities are wide and generous. Its compulsion is upon us.

—Woodrow Wilson

No man was ever endowed with a right without being at the same time saddled with a responsibility.

—Gerald W. Johnson

Those who are unwilling to invest in the future haven't earned one.

—H.W. Lewis, *Technological Risk*, 1990

Dr. Miller says we are pessimistic because life seems like a very bad, very screwed—up film. If you ask "What the hell is wrong with the projector?" and go up to the control room, you find it's empty. You *are* the projectionist, and you should have been up there all the time.

—Colin Wilson

We all participate in weaving the social fabric; we should therefore all participate in patching the fabric when it develops holes.

—Anne C. Weisberg, *Everything a Working Mother Needs to Know*, 1994

We are made wise not by the recollection of our past, but by the responsibility for our future.

—George Bernard Shaw

A hundred times every day I remind myself that my inner and outer life are based on the labors of other men, living and dead, and that I must exert myself in order to give in the same measure as I have received and am still receiving.

—Albert Einstein

If I knew something useful to me and harmful to my family, I should put it out of my mind. If I knew something useful to my family and not to my country, I should try to forget it. If I knew something useful to my country and harmful to Europe, or useful to Europe and harmful to the human race, I should consider it a crime.

—Montesquieu

There is a mysterious cycle in human events. To some generations much is given. Of other generations much is expected.

—Franklin D. Roosevelt

(The earth) belongs as much to those who are to come after us, and whose names are already written in the book of creation, as to us; and we have no right, by anything that we do or neglect, to involve them in unnecessary penalties, or deprive them of benefits which it was in our power to bequeath.

—John Ruskin

The eyes of all people are upon us. Soe that if we shall deal falsely with our God in this work we have undertaken, and so cause him to withdraw his present help from us, we shall be made a story and a byword throughout the world.

—John Winthrop

REVOLUTION

... I am proud this morning to salute you as fellow revolutionaries. Neither you nor I are willing to accept the tyranny of poverty, nor the dictatorship of ignorance, nor the despotism of ill health, nor the oppression of bias and prejudice and bigotry. We want change. We want progress. We want it both abroad and at home—and we aim to get it.

—Lyndon B. Johnson

Those who make peaceful revolution impossible will make violent revolution inevitable.

—John F. Kennedy

... we live in an era of revolution—the revolution of rising expectations.

—Adlai E Stevenson

RIGHTS

Still, if you will not fight for the right when you can easily win without bloodshed; if you will not fight when your victory will be sure and not too costly; you may come to the moment when you will have to fight with all the odds against you and only a precarious chance of survival. There may even be a worse case. You may have to fight when there is no hope of victory, because it is better to perish than live as slaves.

—Winston Churchill

You may burn my body to ashes, and scatter them to the winds of heaven; you may drag my soul down to the regions of darkness and despair to be tormented forever; but you will never get me to support a measure which I believe to be wrong, although by doing so I may accomplish that which I believe to be right.

—Attributed to Abraham Lincoln

Stand with anybody that stands *right*. Stand with him while he is right and part with him when he goes wrong.

—Abraham Lincoln

Let us not be content to wait and see what will happen, but give us the determination to make the right things happen.

—Peter Marshall

Aggressive fighting for the right is the noblest sport the world affords.

—Theodore Roosevelt

My country, right or wrong; if right, to be kept right; and if wrong, to be set right.

—Carl Schurz

SEA

I have seen the sea lashed into fury and tossed into spray, and its grandeur moves the soul of the dullest man; but I remember that it is not the billows, but the calm level of the sea from which all heights and depths are measured.

—James A. Garfield

As they say … a rising tide lifts all the boats. And a partnership, by definition, serves both partners, without domination or unfair advantage.

—John F. Kennedy

SEX

I don't see why we can't get along just as well with a polygamist who doesn't polyg as we do with a lot of monogamists who don't monog!

—Attributed to Boies Penrose

I lose my respect for the man who can make the mystery of sex the subject of a coarse jest, yet when you speak earnestly and seriously on the subject, is silent.

—Henry David Thoreau

The state has no business in the bedrooms of the nation.

—Pierre Trudeau

Remember, if you smoke after sex you're doing it too fast.

—Woody Allen

Anybody who believes that the way to a man's heart is through his stomach flunked geography.

—Robert Byrne, quoted in *1,911 Best Things Anybody Ever Said*, 1988

The tragedy of sexual intercourse is the perpetual virginity of the soul.

—William B. Yeats

Sex on television can't hurt you unless you fall off.

—Author Unknown

Condoms aren't completely safe. A friend of mine was wearing one and got hit by a bus.

—Bob Rubin

Flies spread disease — keep yours zipped.

—Author Unknown

The best contraceptive is the word *no* — repeated frequently.

—Margaret Smith

Don't knock masturbation — it's sex with someone I love.

—Woody Allen

For the first time in history, sex is more dangerous than the cigarette afterward.

—Jay Leno

Sex is not the answer. Sex is the question. "Yes" is the answer.

—Swami X

Men get laid, but women get screwed.

—Quentin Crisp

It is bad enough that people are dying of AIDS, but no one should die of ignorance.

—Elizabeth Taylor

When a guy goes to a hooker, he's not paying her for sex, he's paying her to leave.

—Author Unknown

A dirty book is rarely dusty.

—Author Unknown

Sex, in America an obsession. In other parts of the world, a fact.

—Marlene Dietrich

When a man talks dirty to a woman, it's sexual harassment. When a woman talks dirty to a man, it's $3.95 a minute.

—Author Unknown

Life in Lubbock, Texas, taught me two things: One is that God loves you and you're going to burn in hell. The other is that sex is the most awful, filthy thing on earth and you should save it for someone you love.

—Butch Hancock

To hear many religious people talk, one would think God created the torso, head, legs and arms, but the devil slapped on the genitals.

—Don Schrader

The best sex education for kids is when Daddy pats Mommy on the fanny when he comes home from work.

—William H. Masters

Contraceptives should be used on every conceivable occasion.

—Spike Milligan

There are three possible parts to a date, of which at least two must be offered: entertainment, food, and affection. It is customary to begin a series of dates with a great deal of entertainment, a moderate amount of food, and the merest suggestion of affection. As the amount of affection increases, the entertainment can be reduced proportionately. When the affection *is* the entertainment, we no longer call it dating. Under no circumstances can the food be omitted.

—Miss Manners' Guide to Excruciatingly Correct Behaviour

No matter how much cats fight, there always seem to be plenty of kittens.

—Abraham Lincoln

My reaction to porn films is as follows: After the first ten minutes, I want to go home and screw. After the first 20 minutes, I never want to screw again as long as I live.

—Erica Jong, *Playboy Magazine*, September 1975

Familiarity breeds contempt — and children.

—Mark Twain, *Notebooks*, 1935

Why do they put the Gideon Bibles only in the bedrooms, where it's usually too late, and not in the barroom downstairs?

—Christopher Morley

We all worry about the population explosion, but we don't worry about it at the right time.

—Arthur Hoppe

What is commonly called love, namely the desire of satisfying a voracious appetite with a certain quantity of delicate white human flesh.

—Henry Fielding

Sex is God's joke on human beings.

—Bette Davis

Love is the answer, but while you are waiting for the answer, sex raises some pretty good questions.

—Woody Allen

Against diseases here the strongest fence
Is the defensive vertue, Abstinence.

—Robert Herrick, "*Abstinence*"

Life without sex might be safer but it would be unbearably dull. It is the sex instinct which makes women seem beautiful, which they are once in a blue moon, and men seem wise and brave, which they never are at all. Throttle it, denaturalize it, take it away, and human existence would be reduced to the prosaic, laborious, boresome, imbecile level of life in an anthill.

—Henry Louis Mencken

AIDS obliges people to think of sex as having, possibly, the direst consequences: suicide. Or murder.

—Susan Sontag

There is nothing wrong with going to bed with someone of your own sex. People should be very free with sex, they should draw the line at goats.

—Elton John

There's nothing better than good sex. But bad sex? A peanut butter and jelly sandwich is better than bad sex.

—Billy Joel

Sex without love is merely healthy exercise.

—Robert Heinlein

The good thing about masturbation is that you don't have to get dressed up for it.

—Truman Capote

It is now quite lawful for a Catholic woman to avoid pregnancy by a resort to mathematics, though she is still forbidden to resort to physics or chemistry.

—H.L. Mencken, *Notebooks*, 1956

Sex relieves tension — love causes it.

—Woody Allen

If you use the electric vibrator near water, you will come and go at the same time.

—Louise Sammons

Men wake up aroused in the morning. We can't help it. We just wake up and we want you. And the women are thinking, "How can he want me the way I look in the morning?" It's because we can't see you. We have no blood anywhere near our optic nerve.

—Andy Rooney

I think I could fall madly in bed with you.

—Author Unknown

Whoever called it necking was a poor judge of anatomy.

—Groucho Marx

Sex is emotion in motion.

—Mae West

Love's mysteries in souls do grow,
But yet the body is his book.

—John Donne, *Extasy*

Why should we take advice on sex from the pope? If he knows anything about it, he shouldn't!

—George Bernard Shaw

I thank God I was raised Catholic, so sex will always be dirty.

—John Waters

For women the best aphrodisiacs are words. The G—spot is in the ears. He who looks for it below there is wasting his time.

—Isabel Allende

Sex without love is an empty experience, but as empty experiences go it's one of the best.

—Woody Allen

Sex between a man and a woman can be absolutely wonderful — provided you get between the right man and the right woman.

—Woody Allen

Literature is mostly about having sex and not much about having children; life is the other way around.

—David Lodge, *The British Museum Is Falling Down*, 1965

Masturbation: the primary sexual activity of mankind. In the nineteenth century it was a disease; in the twentieth, it's a cure.

—Thomas Szasz

We have reason to believe that man first walked upright to free his hands for masturbation.

—Lily Tomlin

An intellectual is a person who's found one thing that's more interesting than sex.

—Aldous Huxley

The big difference between sex for money and sex for free is that sex for money usually costs less.

—Brendan Francis, *Playboy*, 1985

The art of procreation and the members employed therein are so repulsive, that if it were not for the beauty of the faces and the adornments of the actors and the pent-up impulse, nature would lose the human species.

—Leonardo da Vinci

I know nothing about sex, because I was always married.

—Zsa Zsa Gabor

If it's not a headboard it's just not worth it.

—Rachel on *Friends*, talking about people bumping their heads

Desire is in men a hunger, in women only an appetite.

—Mignon McLaughlin, *The Neurotic's Notebook*, 1960

The hypothalamus is one of the most important parts of the brain, involved in many kinds of motivation, among other functions. The hypothalamus controls the "Four F's": fighting, fleeing, feeding, and mating.

—Unknown psychology professor in neuropsychology course

Sex at age ninety is like trying to shoot pool with a rope.

—George Burns

It is not sex that gives the pleasure, but the lover.

—Marge Piercy

A chicken and an egg are lying in bed. The chicken is smoking a cigarette with a satisfied smile on its face and the egg is frowning and looking put out. The egg mutters to no one in particular, "I guess we answered *that* question."

—Author Unknown

Love is a matter of chemistry, but sex is a matter of physics.

—Author Unknown

Sex got me into trouble from the age of fifteen: I'm hoping that by the time I'm seventy I'll straighten it out.

—Harold Robbins

Nymphomaniac: a woman as obsessed with sex as an average man.

—Mignon McLaughlin, *The Neurotic's Notebook*, 1960

Conservatives say teaching sex education in the public schools will promote promiscuity. With our education system? If we promote promiscuity the same way we promote math or science, they've got nothing to worry about.

—Beverly Mickins

Nature abhors a virgin — a frozen asset.

—Clare Booth Luce

A widespread taste for pornography means that nature is alerting us to some threat of extinction.

—J.G. Ballard, "News from the Sun," *Myths of the Near Future*, 1982

You know, of course, that the Tasmanians, who never committed adultery, are now extinct.

—W. Somerset Maugham, *The Bread-Winner*

It is not economical to go to bed early to save the candles if the result is twins.

—Chinese Proverb

Chastity: The most unnatural of the sexual perversions.

—Aldous Huxley, *Eyeless in Gaza*, 1936

He no play—da—game. He no make—a—da rules!

—Earl Butz, referring to the Pope's stricture against contraception

Obscenity is whatever gives the Judge an erection.

—Author Unknown

The only thing wrong with being an atheist is that there's nobody to talk to during an orgasm.

—Author Unknown

Out upon it, I have lov'd
Three whole days together;
And am like to love three more,

If it prove fair weather.

—John Suckling

Love ain't nothing, but sex misspelled.

—Harlan Ellison

Being with a woman all night never hurt no professional baseball player. It's staying up all night looking for a woman that does him in.

—Casey Stengel

Sex: the pleasure is momentary, the position ridiculous and the expense damnable.

—Lord Chesterfield

Virginity can be lost by a thought.

—St. Jerome

The tragedy is, when you've got sex in the head, instead of down where it belongs.

—D.H. Lawrence

Men reach their sexual peak at eighteen. Women reach theirs at thirty-five. Do you get the feeling that God is playing a practical joke?

—Rita Rudner

Pornography is supposed to arouse sexual desires. If pornography is a crime, when will they arrest makers of perfume?

—Richard Fleischer

Instruction in sex is as important as instruction in food; yet not only are our adolescents not taught the physiology of sex, but never warned that the strongest sexual attraction may exist between persons so incompatible in tastes and capacities that they could not endure living together for a week much less a lifetime.

—George Bernard Shaw, *Everybody's Political What's What*, 1944

Were kisses all the joys in bed,
One woman would another wed.

—William Shakespeare, *Sonnets to Sundry Notes of Music, IV*

Sex is the great amateur art. The professional, male or female, is frowned on: he or she misses the point, and spoils the show.

—David Cort

The best contraceptive is a glass of cold water: not before or after, but instead.

—Author Unknown

Having sex is like playing bridge. If you don't have a good partner, you'd better have a good hand.

—Author Unknown

Isn't it interesting how the sounds are the same for an awful nightmare and great sex?

—From the television show *The Golden Girls*

I want to tell you a terrific story about oral contraception. I asked this girl to sleep with me and she said 'No.'

—Woody Allen

Vanity, revenge, loneliness, boredom, all apply: lust is one of the least of the reasons for promiscuity.

—Mignon McLaughlin, *The Second Neurotic's Notebook*, 1966

Don't worry, it only seems kinky the first time.

—Author Unknown

The reproduction of mankind is a great marvel and mystery. Had God consulted me in the matter, I should have advised him to continue the generation of the species by fashioning them out of clay.

—Martin Luther

What they love to yield they would often rather have stolen. Rough seduction delights them, the boldness of near rape is a compliment.

—Ovid, *The Art of Love*

When a man goes on a date he wonders if he is going to get lucky. A woman already knows.

—Frederike Ryder

My father told me all about the birds and the bees, the liar — I went steady with a woodpecker till I was twenty-one.

—Bob Hope

Do infants enjoy infancy as much as adults enjoy adultery?

—Author Unknown

I once knew a woman who offered her honor
So I honored her offer
And all night long I was on her and off her.

—Author Unknown

Those who have prophesied dreadful consequences as a result of the greater sexual freedom which the young assert — unwanted babies, venereal disease and so on — are usually the very same people who seek the fulfillment of their prophecies by opposing the free availability to the young of contraception and the removal of the stigma and mystification that surround venereal disease.

—Colin Ward, *Anarchy in Action*

An erection is like the Theory of Relativity — the more you think about it, the harder it gets.

—Author Unknown

Men are those creatures with two legs and eight hands.

—Jayne Mansfield

I'm all for bringing back the birch, but only between consenting adults.

—Gore Vidal

When the history of civilization is written, it will be a biological history and Margaret Sanger will be its heroine.

—H.G. Wells, 1935

The difference between light and hard is that you can sleep with a light on.

—Author Unknown

Kinky is using a feather. Perverted is using the whole chicken.

—Author Unknown

Tell him I've been too fucking busy — or vice versa.

—Dorothy Parker

My cock doesn't talk politics.

—S. Sachs

I think men talk to women so they can sleep with them and women sleep with men so they can talk to them.

—Jay McInerney

I'd like to meet the man who invented sex and see what he's working on now.

—Author Unknown

A student undergoing a word-association test was asked why a snowstorm put him in mind of sex. He replied frankly: "Because everything does."

—Honor Tracy

How lucky we are that we can reach our genitals instead of that spot on our back that itches.

—Flash Rosenberg

The difference between pornography and erotica is lighting.

—Gloria Leonard

Its avowed purpose is to excite sexual desire, which, I should have thought, is unnecessary in the case of the young, inconvenient in the case of the middle aged, and unseemly in the old.

—Malcolm Muggeridge, on pornography, *Tread Softly For You Tread On My Jokes*, 1966

Sex is interesting, but it's not totally important. I mean it's not even as important (physically) as excretion. A man can go seventy years without a piece of ass, but he can die in a week without a bowel movement.

—Charles Bukowski, *Notes on a Dirty Old Man*

When authorities warn you of the sinfulness of sex, there is an important lesson to be learned. Do not have sex with the authorities.

—Matt Groening

There are a number of mechanical devices which increase sexual arousal, particularly in women. Chief among these is the Mercedes—Benz 380SL convertible.

—P.J. O'Rourke

I regret to say that we of the FBI are powerless to act in cases of oral—genital intimacy, unless it has in some way obstructed inter-state commerce.

—Attributed to J. Edgar Hoover,

Pornography is the attempt to insult sex, to do dirt on it.

—D.H. Lawrence

I'm not cheap, but I am on special this week.

—Author Unknown

Love is not the dying moan of a distant violin — it's the triumphant twang of a bedspring.

—S.J. Perelman

It doesn't matter what you do in the bedroom as long as you don't do it in the street and frighten the horses.

—Mrs. Patrick Campbell

A woman occasionally is quite a serviceable substitute for masturbation.

—Karl Kraus

Never let the little head do the thinking for the big head.

—Author unknown, advice to teenage boys, quoted in *Friendly Advice* compiled by Jon Winokur

Our love could change the orbit of the earth. So, if a meteor ever comes hurtling towards earth with the guarantee of destruction, top scientists may call on us to, well, you know, do it like crazy for the sake of humankind.

—Author Unknown

Nothing risqué, nothing gained.

—Alexander Woollcott

To succeed with the opposite sex, tell her you're impotent. She can't wait to disprove it.

—Cary Grant

My message to the businessman of this country when they go abroad on business is that there is one thing above all they can take with them to stop them catching AIDS, and that is the wife.

—Edwina Currie, *The Observer*, 15 February 1987

[T]he common thread that binds nearly all animal species seems to be that males are willing to abandon all sense and decorum, even to risk their lives, in the frantic quest for sex.

—Randy Thornhill and Craig T. Palmer, *A Natural History of Rape*

Now, if groups like Moral Majority have their way, there won't be any sex education at school, and our kids will be the dumbest in the world when it comes to sex.... But our parents are sexually retarded too.... Fear and primitive morals are creating a sexual pressure cooker in this country and soon the top will blow.... Only in the U.S. do we find children drawing a picture of a baby coming from the clouds or from under a cabbage leaf.

—Dr. Floyd Martinson

SHAKESPEARE

Others abide our question, Thou art free.
We ask and ask; Thou smilest and art still,
Out—topping knowledge,

—Matthew Arnold, *Shakespeare*

Shakespeare!—to such names sounding, what succeeds Fitly as silence?

—R. Browning, *The Names*

Shake was a dramatist of note;
He lived by writing things to quote,

—H. AndC. Bunner,.Shake, *Mulleary and Go—ethe*

Our *myriad—minded* Shakespeare—a phrase … which belongs to him, *dejure singulari, et ex priuilegio naturae.*

—S. T. Coleridge, *Biographia Literaria*

Subtract from many modern poets all that may be found in Shakespeare, and trash will remain,

—C. C. Colton, *Lacon*

But Shakespeare's magic touch could not copied be;
Within that circle none durst walk but he.

—Dryden, Prologue to his version of *The Tempest*

There is an upstart Crow, beautified with our feathers that with his *Tygers heart wrapt in a Players hide* suppose he is as well able to bumbast out a blanke verse as the bes of you; and being an absolute *Johannes factotum*, is, in hi own conceit, the onely Shake—scene In a countrie … .

—Robert Greene, *Groatsworth of Wit* … (1595)

I remember, the players have often mentioned it as a honour to Shakespeare, that in his writing (whatsoever he penn 'd) he never blotted out a line. My answer hath bee would he had blotted out a thousand.

—Ben Jonson, *Explorate*

And Hamlet how boring, how boring to live with,
So mean and self-conscious, blowing and snoring
His wonderful speeches, full of other folks' whoring.

—D. H. Lawrence, *When I Read Shakespeare*

… sweetest Shakespear, fancy's child,
Warble his native wood—notes wild.

—Milton, *L'Allegn*

What needs my Shakespear for his honour'd bones,
The labour of an age in piled stones,
Or that his hallow'd reliques should be hid
Under a star—y pointing pyramid?

—Milton, *On Shakespear*

Shakespeare (whom you and every playhouse bill
Style the divine! the matchless! what you will),
For gain, not glory, wing'd his roving flight,
And grew immortal in his own despite.

—Pope, *Imitations of Horace*

Shakespeare is a savage with sparks of genius which shine in a dreadful darkness of night.

—Voltaire, *Irene* (preliminary letter,

Good frend for Jesvs sake forbeare,
To digg the dust cncloased heare.
Bles be ye man yt spares thes stones.
And curst be he yt moves my bones.

—Epitaph on Shakespeare's tombstone in Stratford

SLUMBER

"Laugh and the world laughs with you, snore and you sleep alone."
—Mrs. Patrick Campbell

If you would relish food, labor for it before you take it; if you enjoy clothing, pay for it before you wear it; if you would sleep soundly, take a clear conscience to bed with you.
—Benjamin Franklin

SOCIETY

Ermined and minked and Persian—lambed,
Be—puffed (be—painted, too, alas!)
Be—decked, be—diamond—be—damned!
The Women of the Better Class.
—Oliver Herford, *The Women of the Better Class*

There are only about four hundred people in New 'fork Society.
—Ward Mcallister (1892,: origin of "The Four Hundred")

There is One great society alone on ear"
The noble Living and the noble Dead.
—Wordsworth *The Prelude, II*

What is the use of a house if you haven't got a tolerable planet to put it on?
—Henry David Thoreau

It's a sad and stupid thing to have to proclaim yourself a revolutionary just to be a decent man.
—David Harris

One of the misfortunes of our time is that in getting rid of false shame, we have killed off so much real shame as well.
—Louis Kronenberger, *Company Manners*, 1954

We do not have to visit a madhouse to find disordered minds; our planet is the mental institution of the universe.

—Johann Wolfgang von Goethe

I think we risk becoming the best informed society that has ever died of ignorance.

—Reuben Blades

Most people are awaiting Virtual Reality; I'm awaiting virtuous reality.

—Eli Khamarov, "Lives of the Cognoscenti"

It'll be a great day when education gets all the money it wants and the Air Force has to hold a bake sale to buy bombers.

—Unknown author, quoted in *You Said a Mouthful* edited by Ronald D. Fuchs

If you're not outraged, you're not paying attention.

—Author Unknown

I think God's going to come down and pull civilization over for speeding.

—Steven Wright

Our modern society is engaged in polishing and decorating the cage in which man is kept imprisoned.

—Swami Nirmalananda, *Enlightened Anarchism*

Do not waste your time on Social Questions. What is the matter with the poor is Poverty; what is the matter with the rich is Uselessness.

—George Bernard Shaw, *Maxims for Revolutionists*

Our democratic capitalist society has converted Eros into an employee of Mammon.

—Octavio Paz

The first gold star a child gets in school for the mere performance of a needful task is its first lesson in graft.

—Philip Wylie, *Generation of Vipers*, 1942

The trouble with the rat race is that even if you win, you're still a rat.

—Lily Tomlin

Natives who beat drums to drive off evil spirits are objects of scorn to smart Americans who blow horns to break up traffic jams.

—Mary Ellen Kelly

Are right and wrong convertible terms, dependant upon popular opinion?

—William Lloyd Garrison

Society is composed of two great classes — those who have more dinners than appetite, and those who have more appetite than dinners.

—Sébastien—Roch Nicholas de Chamfort

A people that values its privileges above its principles soon loses both.

—Dwight D. Eisenhower, first inaugural address, 20 January 1953

It is the safest of times, it is the riskiest of times.... What the Dickens is going on here?

—Denton Morrison, on chemicals, technology, and risk, quoted in National Academy of Sciences, Improving Risk Communication, 1989

Few great men could pass Personnel.

—Paul Goodman, *Growing Up Absurd: Problems of Youth in the Organized Society*, 1956

You're obliged to pretend respect for people and institutions you think absurd. You live attached in a cowardly fashion to moral and social conventions you despise, condemn, and know lack all foundation. It is that permanent contradiction between your ideas and desires and all the dead formalities and vain pretenses of your civilization which makes you sad, troubled and unbalanced. In that intolerable conflict you lose all joy of life and all feeling of personality, because at every moment they suppress and restrain and check the free play of your powers. That's the poisoned and mortal wound of the civilized world.

—Octave Mirbeau, *Torture Garden*, "The Mission," Chapter 8

Pharmaceutical companies will soon rule the world if we keep letting them believe that we are a happy, functional society so long as all the women are on Prozac, all children on Ritalin, and all men on Viagra.

—The Quote Garden

It would be a service to mankind if the pill were available in slot machines and the cigarette were placed on prescription.

—Malcolm Potts, MD

There is no hope for a civilization which starts each day to the sound of an alarm clock.

—Author Unknown

Suburbia is where the developer bulldozes out the trees, then names the streets after them.

—Bill Vaughn

The time is ripe, and rotten—ripe, for change.

—Lowell

Perhaps in time the so called Dark Ages will be thought of as including our own.

—Georg Christoph Lichtenberg

The danger of the past was that men became slaves. The danger of the future is that man may become robots.

—Erich Fromm

We create an environment where it is alright to hate, to steal, to cheat, and to lie if we dress it up with symbols of respectability, dignity and love.

—Whitney Moore, Jr.

When people go to work, they shouldn't have to leave their hearts at home.

—Betty Bender

Widespread caffeine use explains a lot about the twentieth century.

—Greg Egan, "*Distress*"

In these times you have to be an optimist to open your eyes when you awake in the morning.

—Carl Sandburg, *New York Post*, 9 September 1960

Oh, for the good old days when people would stop Christmas shopping when they ran out of money.

—Author Unknown

Most of the change we think we see in life
Is due to truths being in and out of favor.

—Robert Frost, "The Black Cottage," *North of Boston*, 1914

Where is the wisdom we have lost in knowledge?
Where is the knowledge we have lost in information?

—T.S. Eliot, *Choruses from The Rock*

Today the world changes so quickly that in growing up we take leave not just of youth but of the world we were young in.

—Peter Medawar

Choice has always been a privilege of those who could afford to pay for it.

—Ellen Frankfort

You can't make up anything anymore. The world itself is a satire. All you're doing is recording it.

—Art Buchwald

Those persons who are burning to display heroism may rest assured that the course of social evolution will offer them every opportunity.

—Havelock Ellis

The trouble with our age is that it is all signposts and no destination.

—*The War Cry*

It isn't so much that hard times are coming; the change observed is mostly soft times going.

—Groucho Marx

We have produced a world of contented bodies and discontented minds.

—Adam Clayton Powell, *Keep the Faith, Baby!*, 1967

Think what a better world it would be if we all, the whole world, had cookies and milk about three o'clock every afternoon and then lay down on our blankets for a nap.

—Barbara Jordan

The world has achieved brilliance without conscience.

—Omar Bradley

Speed kills colour … the gyroscope, when turning at full speed, shows up gray.

—Paul Morand

We are living in a world today where lemonade is made from artificial flavors and furniture polish is made from real lemons.

—Alfred E. Newman

The thoughts of Plato and Machiavelli … don't seem quite enough armor for a world beset with splitting the atoms, urban guerrillas, nineteen varieties of psychotherapists, amplified guitars, napalm, computers, astronauts, and an atmosphere polluted simultaneously with auto exhaust and TV commercials.

—John Fischer

Nothing can be more readily disproved than the old saw, "You can't keep a good man down." Most human societies have been beautifully organized to keep good men down.

—John W. Gardner

The trouble with our times is that the future is not what it used to be.

—Paul Valery

What's wrong with this world is, it's not finished yet. It is not competed to the point where man can put his final signature to the job and say, "It is finished. We made it and it works."

—William Faulkner, address, Wellesley, Massachusetts, 8 June 1952

Most people are willing to pay more to be amused than to be educated.

—Robert C. Savage, *Life Lessons*

When we think of the past, we forget the fools and remember the sage. We reverse the process for our own time.

—George Boas

Yes, I am positive that one of the great curatives of our evils, our maladies, social, moral, and intellectual, would be a return to the soil, a rehabilitation of the work of the fields.

—Charles Wagner

Commuter — one who spends his life
In riding to and from his wife;
A man who shaves and takes a train,
And then rides back to shave again.

—E.B. White, "The Commuter," *Poems and Sketches*, 1982

Unhappy is a people that has run out of words to describe what is going on.

—Thurman Arnold

You taught me to be nice, so nice that now I am so full of niceness, I have no sense of right and wrong, no outrage, no passion.

—Garrison Keillor

Fame is proof that the people are gullible.

—Ralph Waldo Emerson

I believe that one of the great problems for us as individuals is the depression and the tension resulting from existence in a world which is increasingly less pleasing to the eye.

—Lady Bird Johnson

So long as all the increased wealth which modern progress brings goes but to build up great fortunes, to increase luxury and make sharper the contrast between the House of Have and the House of Want, progress is not real and cannot be permanent.

—Henry George, *Progress and Poverty*, 1879

One of the definitions of sanity is the ability to tell real from unreal. Soon we'll need a new definition.

—Alvin Toffler

The world is so dreadfully managed, one hardly knows to whom to complain.

—Ronald Firbank

We get lost in a fog of abstractions and easily forget that man is a bloodhound sniffing out the real.

—Robert C. Pollock

Failure seems to be regarded as the one unpardonable crime, success as the all-redeeming virtue, the acquisition of wealth as the single worthy aim of life. The hair raising revelations of skullduggery and grand scale thievery merely incite others to surpass by yet bolder outrages and more corrupt combinations.

—Charles Francis Adams

The world is governed more by appearance than realities so that it is fully as necessary to seem to know something as to know it.

—Daniel Webster

Armaments, universal debt and planned obsolescence — those are the three pillars of Western prosperity.

—Aldous Huxley, *Island*

People haven't time to learn anything. They buy things ready made in stores. But since there are no stores where you can buy friends, people no longer have friends.

—Antoine de Saint—Exupéry, *The Little Prince*, 1943, translated from French by Richard Howard

The human race has had long experience and a fine tradition in surviving adversity. But we now face a task for which we have little experience, the task of surviving prosperity.

—Alan Gregg

I never expected to see the day when girls would get sunburned in the places they do now.

—Will Rogers

I don't believe medical discoveries are doing much to advance human life. As fast as we create ways to extend it we are inventing ways to shorten it.

—Christiaan Barnard

Society is always engaged in a vast conspiracy to preserve itself — at the expense of the new demands of each new generation.

—John Haynes Holmes

The age of chivalry is gone. That of sophisters, economists and calculators has succeeded.

—Edmund Burke, *Reflections on the Revolution in France*

[The] men of the technostructure are the new and universal priesthood. Their religion is business success; their test of virtue is growth and profit. Their bible is the computer printout; their communion bench is the committee room.

—J.K. Galbraith, *The Age of Uncertainty*, 1977

If living conditions don't stop improving in this country, we're going to run out of humble beginnings for our great men.

—Russell P. Askue

With each passing year, one has less to say, and knows better how to say it.

—Mignon McLaughlin, *The Second Neurotic's Notebook*, 1966

The things that will destroy America are prosperity-at-any-price, peace-at-any-price, safety-first instead of duty-first, the love of soft living, and the get-rich-quick theory of life.

—Theodore Roosevelt

It is one of the maladies of our age to profess a frenzied allegiance to truth in unimportant matters, to refuse consistently to face her where graver issues are at stake.

—Norman Douglas

There's a standard formula for success in the entertainment medium, and that is: "Beat it to death if it succeeds."

—Ernie Kovacs

[H]istory assures us that civilizations decay quite leisurely.

—Will and Ariel Durant, *Lessons of History*

Usually, terrible things that are done with the excuse that progress requires them are not really progress at all, but just terrible things.

—Russell Baker

Society is now one polished horde,
Formed of two mighty tribes, the Bores and Bored.

—Lord Byron, *Don Juan*

I've been reading a lot lately about Indian captives. One woman who had been captured by the Indians and made a squaw was resentful when she was rescued because she'd found that there was a lot more work to do as the wife of a white man.

—Stephen Vincent Benét

The things that are wrong with the country today are the sum total of all the things that are wrong with us as individuals.

—Charles W. Tobey

The twentieth century seems afflicted by a gigantic … power failure. Powerlessness and the sense of powerlessness may be the environmental disease of the age.

—Russell Baker, New York Times, 1 May 1969

Punishment is now unfashionable … because it creates moral distinctions among men, which, to the democratic mind, are odious. We prefer a meaningless collective guilt to a meaningful individual responsibility.

—Thomas Szasz

The atom bombs are piling up in the factories, the police are prowling through the cities, the lies are streaming from the loudspeakers, but the earth is still going round the sun.

—George Orwell, *Shooting an Elephant*, 1950

The three horrors of modern life — talk without meaning, desire without love, work without satisfaction.

—Mignon McLaughlin, *The Neurotic's Notebook*, 1960

Most of our diversions do not so much delay death as accustom us to it.

—Mignon McLaughlin, *The Second Neurotic's Notebook*, 1966

Once the Xerox copier was invented, private diplomacy died. There's no such thing as secrecy. It's just a question of whether it's leaked or revealed openly.

—Andrew Young

It is madness beyond compare
To try to reform the world.

—Molière, *The Misanthrope*, 1666

The world is changing so fast I've got societal vertigo.

—B.F. Tucson, 1991

The number of substitutes for fine and clean thinking the world provides positively gnaws at one's vitals.

—Harold J. Laski

I think societal instinct much deeper than sex instinct — and societal repression much more devastating.

—D.H. Lawrence

In spite of all our speeding it's still the style to be late.

—Kin Hubbard

Noise, crowding, pollution, and the sheer rush of our complex, modern society are rapidly becoming as oppressive to many individuals as the worst kind of political dictatorship.

—Thomas F. Eagleton

The greater the mental charlatan, the more definite his insistence on the wickedness and weaknesses of human nature. Yet how can anyone speak of it today, with every soul in a prison, with every heart fettered, wounded, and maimed? ... With human nature caged in a narrow space, whipped daily into submission, how can we speak of its potentialities?

—Emma Goldman, *Anarchism*

I am not quite sure what the advantage is in having a few more dollars to spend if the air is too dirty to breathe, the water too polluted to drink, the commuters are losing out in the struggle to get in and out of the city, the streets are filthy, and the schools so bad that the young perhaps wisely stay away, and the hoodlums roll citizens for some of the dollars they saved in the tax cut.

—John Kenneth Galbraith

Beggars should be abolished. It annoys one to give to them, and it annoys one not to give to them.

—Friedrich Wilhelm Nietzsche, "On the Pitying," *Thus Spake Zarathustra*

We have smothered ourselves, buried ourselves, in the vast heap of information which all of us have and none of us has.

—Gamaliel Bradford

I believe ... that security declines as security machinery expands.

—E.B. White

If some people got their rights they would complain of being deprived of their wrongs.

—Oliver Herford

How can a society that exists on instant mashed potatoes, packaged cake mixes, frozen dinners, and instant cameras teach patience to its young?

—Paul Sweeney

Society honors its living conformists and its dead troublemakers.

—Mignon McLaughlin

Final Ruin fiercely drives
Her ploughshare o'er creation.

—Edward Young

Any society that needs disclaimers has too many lawyers.

—Erik Pepke

There are more doctors in a single North Shore medical building than in one entire West Side ghetto.

—Jack Starr

The human race's prospects of survival were considerably better when we were defenceless against tigers than they are today when we have become defenceless against ourselves.

—Arnold Toynbee

Psychoanalysis can provide a theory of 'progress,' but only by viewing history as a neurosis.

—Norman O. Brown, *Life Against Death*

We're the middle children of history.... no purpose or place. We have no Great War, no Great Depression. Our great war is a spiritual war. Our great depression is our lives.

—From the movie *Fight Club*

American youth attributes much more importance to arriving at driver's license age than at voting age.

—Marshall McLuhan, *Understanding Media: The Extensions of*

Man, 1964

You can say this for ready-mixes — the next generation isn't going to have any trouble making pies exactly like mother used to make.

—Earl Wilson

You can find your way across this country using burger joints the way a navigator uses stars.

—Charles Kuralt

If you want a picture of the future, imagine a boot stamping on the human face — forever.

—George Orwell

[A] science is said to be useful if its development tends to accentuate the existing inequalities in the distribution of wealth, or more directly promotes the destruction of human life.

—Harold Hardy Godfrey, *A Mathematician's Apology*, 1941

It's difficult to view the world outside our human context. Staying alive and paying the bills both require our attention squarely fixed on our own business. Our sprawling cities and suburbs are wonderful and frightening tributes to creative self—absorption. In them, we spend our microscheduled days bustling between work and the endless details of our private lives, turning in our moments of rest to the buzzing distractions of television and computers — all accelerating toward some ultimate, unseen fulfillment of convenience and hyperreality. Little encourages us to pause and look around, much less question the end goal of all our busyness. Anything slower than the quick cuts of TV commercials is overwhelmed by our impatience and short attention. Unfortunately, we might be missing something important — to our happiness *and* to our survival. The purpose of this book is to help remind us.

—From the introduction to *The Sacred Earth: Writers on Nature & Spirit*, edited by Jason Gardner, 1998, New World Library

The means by which we live have outdistanced the ends for which we live. Our scientific power has outrun our spiritual power. We have guided missiles and misguided men.

—Martin Luther King, Jr., *Strength to Love*, 1963

Everything is for the eye these days — TV, *Life*, *Look*, the movies. Nothing is just for the mind. The next generation will have eyeballs as big as cantaloupes and no brain at all.

—Fred Allen

Formerly, when religion was strong and science weak, men mistook magic for medicine; now, when science is strong and religion weak, men mistake medicine for magic.

—Thomas Szasz, *The Second Sin*, 1973

The trouble with the laws these days is that criminals know their rights better than their wrongs.

—Author Unknown

Somebody recently figured out that we have 35 million laws to enforce the ten commandments.

—Attributed to both Bert Masterson and Earl Wilson

In the lifetime of one person, we went from figuring out where we came from to figuring out how to get rid of ourselves.

—Jack Horner, on the eighty years between Darwin's *On the Origin of Species* and the nuclear bomb, in *Time*, 26 April 1993

Death is losing its terror. It is the emergency exit for a world that is becoming more frightening death ever was.

—Julian Green, *Diary*, 28 December 1958

Scientific discovery consists in the interpretation for our own convenience of a system of existence which has been made with no eye to our convenience at all.

—Norbert Wiener, *The Human Use of Human Beings*, 1950

Science is now the craft of the manipulation, substitution and deflection of the forces of nature. What I see coming is a gigantic slaughterhouse, an Auschwitz, in which valuable enzymes, hormones, and so on will be extracted instead of gold teeth.

—Erwin Chargaff, *Columbia Forum*, Summer 1969

I always turn to the sports section first. The sports section records people's accomplishments; the front page nothing but man's failures.

—Earl Warren, quoted in *Sports Illustrated*, 22 July 1968

It seems a long time since the morning mail could be called correspondence.

—Jacques Barzun, *God's Country and Mine*, 1954

Our current obsession with creativity is the result of our continued striving for immortality in an era when most people no longer believe in an afterlife.

—Arianna Stassinopoulos

Progress imposes not only new possibilities for the future but new restrictions.

—Norbert Wiener, *The Human Use of Human Beings*, 1950

Jefferson thought schools would produce free men: we prove him right by putting dropouts in jail.

—Benjamin R. Barber

Man is the animal that intends to shoot himself out into interplanetary space, after having given up on the problem of an efficient way to get himself five miles to work and back each day.

—Bill Vaughan

If our American way of life fails the child, it fails us all.

—Pearl S. Buck

This strange disease of modern life, with its sick hurry, its divided aims.

—Matthew Arnold

In this prostituting society, we all have to hustle, and I'd rather suck cock than kiss ass!

— Attributed to Margo St. James

The quintessential revolution is that of the spirit, born of an intellectual conviction of the need for change in those mental attitudes and values which shape the course of a nation's development. A revolution which aims merely at changing official policies and institutions with a view to an improvement in material conditions has little chance of genuine success. Without a revolution in spirit, the forces which had produced inequities of the old order would continue to be operative, posing a constant threat to the process of reform and regeneration. It is not enough merely to call for freedom, democracy and human rights. There has to be a united determination to persevere in the struggle, to make sacrifices in the name of enduring truths, to resist the corrupting influences of desire, ill will, ignorance, and fear.

—Aung San Suu Kyi

We have a system that increasingly taxes work and subsidizes nonwork.

—Milton Friedman

There is more to life than increasing its speed.

—Mohandas K. Gandhi

SONG

I cannot sing the old songs
I sang long years ago,
For heart and voice would fail me
And foolish tears would flow.

—Charlotte A. Barnard, *I Cannot Sing the Old Songs*

Sing me the songs I delighted to hear
Long, long ago, long ago.

—T. H. Bayly, *The Long Ago*

That which is not worth saying is sung.

—Beaumarchais, *Barber of Seville*

A wandering minstrel I—
A thing of shreds and patches,
Of ballads, songs, and snatches,
And dreamy lullaby.

—W. S. Gilbert, *The Mikado, I*

It's the song of a merryman, moping mum,
Whose soul was sad, and whose glance was glum,
Who sipped no sup, and who craved no crumb
As he sighed for the love of a ladye.

—W. S. Gilbert, Yeomen *of the Guard, I*

Because the road was steep and long
And through a dark and lonely land,
God set upon my lips a song
And put a lantern in my hand,

—Joyce Kilmer, *Love's Lantern*

In Heaven a spirit doth dwell
Whose heart—strings are a lute—
None sing so wildly well As the angel Israfel.
—Poe, Israfel

Singing is sweet, but be sure of this,
Lips only sing when they cannot kiss.
—James Thomson ("B, V,"), *Sunday Up the River*

SONGS, OLD AND POPULAR

Abdul the Bulbul
The sons of the prophet are brave men and bold,
And quite unaccustomed to fear,
But the bravest by far in the ranks of the Shah
Was Abdul the Bulbul Amir.
—Anon. (college song in America)

After the Ball
Many a heart is aching, if you could read them all,
Many the hopes that have vanished, after the ball.
—Charles K. Harris (1892)

Bananas
Yes, we have no bananas,
We have no bananas today.
—F. Silver And I. Cohen (1923)

Bring Back My *Bonnie to Me*
My Bonnie lies over the ocean,
My Bonnie lies over the sea,
My Bonnie lies over the ocean,
Oh, bring back my Bonnie to me.
—Anon. (1882)

The Camptown Races

De Camptown ladies sing dis song
Doodah! doodah!
De Camptown race track five miles long
Oh! Doodah—day!
I come down dah wid my hat caved in
Doodah! doodah!
I go back home wid a pocket full o' tin
Oh! Doodah—day!

Captain Jinks

I'm Captain Jinks of the Horse Marines,
I often live beyond my means;
I sport young ladies in their teens,
To cut a swell in the army.
—William Lindgard (1869)

Clementine

In a cavern, in a canyon,
Excavating for a mine,
Dwelt a miner, forty niner,
And his daughter, Clementine.
Oh my darling, oh my darling,
Oh my darling Clementine
You are lost and gone forever
Oh my darling Clementine.
—Percy Montross (1880)

Come Home, Father

Father, dear Father, come home with me now!
The clock in the steeple strikes one.
You said you were coming right home from the shop

As soon as your day's work was done.
—Henry Clay Work (1862)

The Curse of an Aching, Heart
You made me what I am to—day,
I hope you're satisfied ...
And though you're not true,
May God bless you.
That's the curse of an aching heart,
—Henry Fink (1913)

Dixie
I wish I was in the land of cotton,
Old times thar are not forgotten,
Look away, look away,
Look away, Dixie land.
In Dixie land whar I was born in,
Early on a frosty mornin'
Look away, look away,
Look away, Dixie land.
Den I wish I was in Dixie,
Hooray, hooray!
In Dixie land we'll take our stand
To lib and die in Dixie.
Away, away,
Away down South in Dixie
Away, away,
Away down South in Dixie.
—Dan Emmett

Father And I Went Down to Camp (Yankee Doodle)
Father and I went down to camp
Along with Captain Goodling,

And there we saw the men and boys,
As thick as hasty pudding.
Yankee Doodle keep it up,
Yankee Doodle dandy
Mind the music and the step,
And with the girls be handy,

—Anon

Go Down, Moses
When Israel was in Egyp' Lan',
Let my people go,
Oppressed so hard they could not stan',
Let my people go.

—Anon

Goodnight Ladies (Merrily We Roll Along)
Goodnight ladies, goodnight ladies,
Goodnight ladies we're gonna leave you now
Merrily we roll along, roll along, roll along,
Merrily we roll along, o'er the deep blue sea.

—Anon.

Hail! Hail! (to a tune from *The Pirates of Penzance)*
Hail! Haill the gang's all here,
What the hell do we care,
What the hell do we care?
Hail! Hail! we're full of cheer—
What the hell do we care. Bill!

—D. A. Esrom (1917)

Hello, Central! Give Me Heaven
Hello, Central! give me heaven,
For my mamma's there.

—Charles K, Harris (1901)

A Hot Time in the Old Town To-night

When you hear those bells go ting—a—ling, ...
There'll be a hot time in the old town to—night.
—Joseph Hayden (1896)

I Don't Want to Play in Your yard

I don't want to play in your yard,
I don t like you any more;
You'll be sorry when you see me
Sliding down our cellar door;
You cant holler down our rain—bar'l,
You can't climb our apple—tree,
I don't want to play in your yard
If you wont be good to me.
—Philip Wingatr (1894)

Little Brown Jug

My wife and I lived all alone
In a little brown shack we called our own
She loved beer and I loved rum
Tell you what it was, oh we had fun.

Chorus:
Ha, ha, ha, you and me,
Little Brown Jug how I love thee,
Ha, ha, ha, you and me,
Little Brown Jug how I love thee.
Had I a cow that gave such milk
I would dress her in the finest silk
Feed her on the choicest hay
And I'd milk her twenty times a day,
—Joseph E. Winneb

Chorus:
Loch Lomond
Oh, ye'll tak' the high road an' I'll tak' the low road,
An' I'll be in Scotland afore ye;
But I an' my true love will never meet again
On the bonnie, bonnie banks of Loch Lomond.
—Anon. (old Scotch ballad)

Mademoiselle from Armentieres
A mademoiselle from Armenteers,
She hasn't been kissed in forty years,
Hinky, dinky, par—lee—voo.
— "Red" Rowley (during World War I)

The Man on the Flying Trapeze
Once I was happy, but now I'm forlorn,
Like an old coat that is tatter 'd and torn,
Left in this wide world to fret and to mourn,
Betray'd by a maid in her teens.
Now this girl that I lov'd she was handsome,
And I tried all I knew her to please,
But I never could please her one quarter so well
Like the man on the flying trapeze.
He flies through the air with the greatest of ease,
This daring young man on the flying trapeze;
His figure is handsome, all girls he can please,
And my love he purloined her away,
—George Leybourne (1860)

McGinty
Down went McGinty to the bottom of the say
He must be very wet, for he hasn't come up yet,
But they say his ghost comes round the dock before the break of

day,
Dressed in his best suit of clothes.
—Joseph Flynn (1889)

My Old Kentucky Home
Weep no more, my lady,
Oh! weep no more to—dayl
We will sing one song for the old Kentucky Home,
For the old Kentucky Home far away,
—Stephen C. Foster (C. 1858)

Nobody
I ain't never done nothin' to nobody;
I ain't never got nothin' from nobody;
And until I get somethin' from somebody, sometime,
I don't Intend to do nothin' for nobody, no time.
—Alex Rogers (1905)

The Old Oaken Bucket
How dear to my heart are the scenes of my childhood
When fond recollections present them to view.
The orchard the meadow, the deep tangled wildwood
And each loving spot which my infancy knew.
The wide spreading pond and the mill that stood by it
The bridge and the rock where the cataract fell.
The Old Oaken Bucket, the ironbound bucket,
The moss covered bucket that hung in the well.
The cot of my father, the little house nigh it
And too the old bucket that hung in the well.
The Old Oaken Bucket, the ironbound bucket,
The moss covered bucket that hung in the well.
—Samuel Woodworth

Promise me

Oh, promise me that some day you and I
Will take our love together to some sky
Where we can be alone and faith renew,
And find the hollows where those flowers grew....

—Clement Scott (1888)

Rosary

The hours I spent with thee, dear heart,
Are as a string of pearls to me;
I count them over, every one apart,
My rosary, my rosary.

—R. C. Rogers (C. 1900)

School-days

School days, school-days, dear old golden rule days,
Readin' and 'ritin' and 'rithmetic,
Taught to the tune of a hick'ry stick.

—Will D. Cobb (1907)

Summer Time
(In The Good Old)

In the good old summer time,
In the good old summer time,
Strolling through the shady lanes,
With your baby mine.

—Ren Shields (1902)

Sweet Betsey From Pike

Oh, don't you remember sweet Betsey from Pike,
Who crossed the big mountains with her lover Ike,
With two yoke of cattle, a large yellow dog,

A tall shanghai rooster and one spotted hog.

Chorus:
Singing tooral lal looral lal looral lal la,
Singing toora! lal looral lal looral lal la,
Sing tooral lal looral, sing tooral lal la,
Singing tooral lal looral lal looral lal la.

One evening quite early they camped on the Platte,
'Twas near by the road on a green shady flat,
Where Betsey, sore—footed lay down to repose—
With wonder Ike gazed on that Pike County rose,

—Anon

STATE

It is one of the happy incidents of the federal system that a single courageous State may, if its citizens choose, serve as a laboratory; and try novel social and economic experiments without risk to the rest of the country.

—Louis D. Brandeis

We are gong down the road to stateism. Where we will wind up, no one can tell, but if some of the new programs seriously proposed should be adopted, there is danger that the individual—whether farmer, worker, manufacturer, lawyer, or doctor—will soon be an economic slave pulling an oar in the galley of the state.

—James F. Bymes

The first act by virtue of which the State really constitutes itself the representative of the whole of society—the taking possession of the means of production in the name of society—this is, at the same time, its last independent act as a State.

—Friedrich Engels

... a State cannot be expected to move with the celerity of a private business man; it is enough if it proceeds, in the language of the English Chancery, with all deliberate speed.

—Oliver Wendell Holmes

The church must be reminded that it is not the master or the servant of the state but rather the conscience of the state.

—Martin Luther King Jr.

STATESMAN

When statesmen forsake their own private conscience for the sake of their public duties ... they lead their country by a short route to chaos.

—Robert Bolt

A disposition to preserve, and an ability to improve, taken together, would be my standard of a statesman. Everything else is vulgar in the conception, perilous in the execution.

—Edmund Burke

A great statesman is he who knows when to depart from traditions, as well as when to adhere to them.

—John Stuart Mill

Statesmen have to bend to the collective will of their peoples or be broken.

—Attributed to Woodrow Wilson

A statesman is a successful politician who is dead,

—Thomas B. Reed (quoted by Sen. H. C. Lodge)

A ginooine statesman should be on his guard,
Ef he *must hev* beliefs, not to b'lieve 'em to hard.

—Jr. Lowell, *Biglow Papers,II*

In statesmanship get the formalities right, never mind about the moralities.

—Mark Twain, *Pudd'nhead Wilsons New Calender*

STRIKE

There is no right to strike against the public safety by anybody anywhere, anytime.

—Calvin Coolidge

I am glad to know that there is a system of labour where the laborer can strike if he wants to! I would to God that such a system prevailed all over the world.

—Abraham Lincoln

TEACHER

A teacher affects eternity; he can never tell where his influence stops.

—Henry Adams, *The Education of Henry Adams*

And gladly would he learn and gladly teach.

—Chaucer, *Canterbury Tales,* Prologue

The schools became a scene
Of solemn farce, where Ignorance on stilts,
His cap well lin'd with logic not his own,
With parrot tongue perform'd the scholar's part,
Proceeding soon a graduated dunce.

—Cowper, *The Task, II*

There, in his noisy mansion, skill'd to rule,

The village master taught his little school; ...
Full well they laugh'd, with counterfeited glee,
At all his jokes, for many a joke had he;
Full well the busy whisper circling round,
Convey'd the dismal tidings when he frown'd.

—Goldsmith, *The Deserted Village*

Our American professors like their literature clear, cold, pure, and very dead.

—Sinclair Lewis, Address, Swedish Academy, 1930

The average schoolmaster is and always must be eventially an ass, for how *can* one imagine an intelligent *can* engaging in such puerile an avocation?

—H. L. Mencken, *Prejudices, Series 3*

The Prussian schoolmaster won the battle of Sadowa.

—Von Moltke, Speech, 1874

Those having torches will pass them on to others.

—Plato, *The Republic*

Delightful task! to rear the tender thought,
To teach the young idea how to shoot.

—Thomson, *The Seasons.*

TEARS

It is the wisdom of crocodiles, that shed tears when they would devour.

—Francis Bacon, *Essays*

Every tear from every eye Becomes a babe in eternity.

—Blake, Auguries *of Innocence*

So bright the tear in Beauty's eye,

Love half regrets to kiss it dry,

—Byron, *The Bride of Abydos*

"I weep for you," the Walrus said:
"I deeply sympathize,"
With sobs and tears he sorted out
Those of the largest size,
Holding his pocket—handkerchief
Before his streaming eyes,

—Lewis Carroll, *Through the Looking Glass*

Nothing is lost that's wrought with tears:
The music that you make below
Is now the music of the spheres.

—John Davidson, A *Ballad of Heaven*

Weep not, my wanton, smile upon my knee,
When thou art old there's grief enough for thee.

—Robert Greene, Song from *Menaphon*

She would have made a splendid wife, for crying only made her eyes more bright and tender.

—O. Henry, *Options*

She by the river sat, and sitting there,
She wept, and made it deeper by a tear.

—Herrick, *Upon Julia, Weeping*

My tears must stop, for every drop
Hinders needle and thread—

—Thomas Hood, *The Song of the Shirt*

If you would have me weep, you must feel grief yourself.
(Si vis me ftere, …)

—Horace, *Ars Poetica*

Thrice he assay'd, and thrice, in spite of scorn,
Tears, such as angels weep, burst forth.

—Milton, *Paradise Lost, I*

If you have tears, prepare to shed them now.

—Shakespeare, *Julius Caesar, III, 2*

Tears, idle tears, I know not what they mean,
Tears from the depth of some divine despair
Rise in the heart, and gather to the eyes,
In looking on the happy autumn—fields,
And thinking of the days that are no more.

—Tennyson, *The Princess*

THINK

No problem can withstand the assault of sustained thinking.

—Voltaire

Reading without reflecting is like eating without digesting.

—Edmund Burke

Often the hands will solve a mystery that the intellect has struggled with in vain.

—Carl G. Jung

Never be afraid to sit awhile and think.

—Lorraine Hansberry, *A Raisin in the Sun*

No matter where you go or what you do, you live your entire life within the confines of your head.

—Terry Josephson

Did you ever stop to think, and forget to start again?

—Winnie the Pooh

People demand freedom of speech as a compensation for the freedom of thought which they seldom use.

—Soren Kierkegaard

An idealist is one who, on noticing that roses smell better than a cabbage, concludes that it will also make better soup.

—Henry L. Mencken

Too often we ... enjoy the comfort of opinion without the discomfort of thought.

—John F. Kennedy

Begin challenging your own assumptions. Your assumptions are your windows on the world. Scrub them off every once in awhile, or the light won't come in.

—Alan Alda

I like to think of thoughts as living blossoms borne by the human tree.

—James Douglas

The forceps of our minds are clumsy things and crush the truth a little in the course of taking hold of it.

—H.G. Wells

Our minds are lazier than our bodies.

—François Duc de La Rochefoucauld, *Maxims*, 1678

Invest a few moments in thinking. It will pay good interest.

—Author Unknown

Some people get lost in thought because it's such unfamiliar territory.

—G. Behn

Thinking is like loving and dying. Each of us must do it for himself.

—Josiah Royce

It is well for people who think, to change their minds occasionally in order to keep them clean.

—Luther Burbank

We spend our days in deliberating, and we end them without coming to any resolve.

—L'Estrange

Our job is not to make up anybody's mind, but to open minds and to make the agony of the decision—making so intense you can escape only by thinking.

—Author Unknown

Thinking in its lower grades is comparable to paper money, and in its higher forms it is a kind of poetry.

—Havelock Ellis, *The Dance of Life*, 1923

The average man never really thinks from end to end of his life. The mental activity of such people is only a mouthing of clichés.

—H.L. Mencken, *Prejudices*, 1925

Few people think no more than two or three times a year; I have made an international reputation for myself by thinking once a week.

—George Bernard Shaw

Irons rusts from disuse, stagnant water loses its purity and in cold weather becomes frozen; even so does inaction sap the vigor of the mind.

—Leonardo da Vinci, *Notebooks*, 1508

The world we have created is a product of our thinking; it cannot be changed without changing our thinking.

—Albert Einstein

Brain, *n*: An apparatus with which we think that we think.

—Ambrose Bierce, *The Devil's Dictionary*

At a certain age some people's minds close up; they live on their intellectual fat.

—William Lyon Phelps

No amount of energy will take the place of thought. A strenuous life with its eyes shut is a kind of wild insanity.

—Henry Van Dyke

Tell your friends not to think aloud
Until they swallow.

—Nickelback, "Leader of Men," *The State*

A man is not idle because he is absorbed in thought. There is a visible labor and there is an invisible labor

—Victor Hugo

Sometimes I think and other times I am.

—Paul Valéry, *Variété: Cantiques spirituels*, 1924

Few minds wear out; more rust out.

—Christian N. Bovee

Opinion is that exercise of the human will which helps us to make a decision without information.

—John Erskine

Some people do not become thinkers simply because their memories are too good.

—Friedrich Wilhelm Nietzsche

Men can live without air a few minutes, without water for about two weeks, without food for about two months —and without a new thought for years on end.

—Kent Ruth

Men who borrow their opinions can never repay their debts.

—George Savile, Marquess de Halifax, *Miscellaneous Thoughts and Reflections*

Chi Wen Tzu always thought three times before taking action. Twice would have been quite enough.

—Confucius, *Analects*

Impartial observers from other planets would consider ours an utterly bizarre enclave if it were populated by birds, defined as flying animals, that nevertheless rarely or never actually flew. They would also be perplexed if they encountered in our seas, lakes, rivers, and ponds, creatures defined as swimmers that never did any swimming. But they would be even more surprised to encounter a species defined as a thinking animal if, in fact, the creature very rarely indulged in actual thinking.

—Steve Allen

What luck for rulers, that men do not think.

—Adolph Hitler

[Thinking is] what a great many people think they are doing when they are merely rearranging their prejudices.

—William James

For those who do not think, it is best at least to rearrange their prejudices once in a while.

—Luther Burbank

How wonderful that we have met with a paradox. Now we have some hope of making progress.

—Niels Bohr

You cannot plough a field by turning it over in your mind.

—Author Unknown

He who will not reason is a bigot; he who cannot is a fool; and he who dares not is a slave.

—William Drummond, *Academical Questions*

Ours is the age which is proud of machines that think and suspicious of men who try to.

—Howard Mumford Jones

I think, therefore I am.
(Cogito, ergo sum)

—Descartes, *Principles of Philosophy*

Men of thought, be up and stirring
Night and day:
Sow and seed—withdraw the curtain—
Clear the way,

—Charles Mackay, *Clear the Way*

No thought without phosphorus.

—Jacob Moleschott, *Lehre der Nahrungsmittel*

And which of you with taking thought can add to his stature one cubit?

—New Testament, *Luke, XII, 25*

If I have done the public any service, it is due to patient thought.

—Sir Isaac Newton, Remark to Dr, Bentley

For my thoughts are not your thoughts, neither are your ways my ways.

—Old Testament, *Isaiah, LV, 8*

Man is but a reed, the weakest in nature, but he is a thinking reed.

—Pascal, *Pensees, VI*

It is clear that thought is not free If the profession of certain opinions make it impossible to earn a living.

—Bertrand Russell, *Sceptical Essays*

Give thy thoughts no tongue
Nor any unproportion'd thought his act.

—Shakespeare, *Hamlet, I, 3*

There is nothing either good or bad but thinking make it so.

—Shakespeare, *Hamlet, II, 2*

Yond Cassius has a lean and hungry look;
He thinks too much: such men are dangerous.

—Shakespeare, *Julius Caesar, 1,2*

Break, break, break,
On thy cold gray stones, O Sea!
And I would that my tongue could utter
The Thoughts that arise in me.

—Tennyson, *Break, Break, Break*

Thoughts too deep to be expressed,
And too strong to be suppressed.

—George Wither, *Mistress of Philaret*

To me the meanest flower that blows can give
Thoughts that do often lie too deep for tears.

—Wordsworth, Intimations *of Immortality*

TRUTH

A truth that's told with bad intent
Beats all the lies you can invent.

—Blake, *Auguries of Innocence*

Tis strange but true: for truth is always strange, — Stranger than fiction.

—Byron, *Don Juan*

I like a look of agony,
Because I know it's true;
Men do not sham convulsion,
Nor simulate a throe.

—Emily Dickinson, *Poems, IV*

Mine eyes have seen the glory of the coming of the Lord;
He is trampling out the vintage where the grapes of wrath are stored;
He hath loosed the fateful lightning of his terrible swift sword;
His truth Is marching on.

—Julia Ward Howe, *Battle Hymn of the Republic*

Once to every man and nation comes the moment to decide,
In the strife of Truth with Falsehood, for the good or evil side.

—J. R. Lowell, *The Present Crisis*

Truth forever on the scaffold,
Wrong forever on the throne.

—J. R. Lowell, *The Present Crisis*

Man with his burning soul
Has but an hour of breath
To build a ship of Truth
In which his soul may sail
Sail on the sea of death
For death takes toll
Of beauty, courage, youth,
Of all but Truth.

—John Masefield, *Truth*

Servant of God, well done! well hast thou fought
The better fight, who single hast maintain'd
Against revolted multitudes the cause
Of truth.

—Milton, *Paradise Lost, VI*

I speak truth, not so much as I would, but as much as I dare; and I dare a little more as I grow older.

—Montaigne, *Essays, III*

Pilate saith unto him, "What is truth?" And when he had said this, he went out again unto the Jews.

—New Testament, *John, XVIII, 38*

Ye shall know the truth, and the truth shall make you free.

—New Testament, *John, VIII, I3*

And oftentimes to win us to our harm,
The instruments of darkness tell us truths,
Win us with honest trifles, to betray 's
In deeper consequence.

—Shakespeare, *Macbeth, 1, 3*

To thine own self be true,

And it must follow, as the night the day,
Thou canst not then be false to any man.

—Shakespeare, *Hamlet, I, 3*

My way of Joking is to tell the truth. It's the runniest joke in the world.

—Bernard Shaw, *John Bull's Other Island, II*

Tnith is the most valuable thing we have.
Let as economize it

—Mark Twain, *Pudd'nhead Wilson's Calendar*

If you shut up truth and bury it under the ground, it will but grow, and gather to itself such explosive power that the day It bursts through it will blow up everything in its way.

—Emile Zola, *J' accuse*

Liberty and Union, now and forever, one and inseparable!

—Daniel Webster, Speech. 1830

Ye shall know the truth, and the truth shall make you mad.

—Aldous Huxley

It is error alone which needs the support of government. Truth can stand by itself.

—Thomas Jefferson, *Notes on Virginia*

I never dreamed of being Shakespeare or Goethe, and I never expected to hold the great mirror of truth up before the world; I dreamed only of being a little pocket mirror, the sort that a woman can carry in her purse; one that reflects small blemishes, and some great beauties, when held close enough to the heart.

—Peter Altenberg

The greatest enemy of any one of our truths may be the rest of our truths.

—William James

Men ardently pursue truth, assuming it will be angels' bread when found.

—W. MacNeile Dixon

There is no god higher than truth.

—Mahatma Gandhi

Truth has very few friends and those few are suicides.

—Author Unknown

It will never be possible by pure reason to arrive at some absolute truth.

—Werner Heisenberg, *Physics and Philosophy*

When I tell any truth, it is not for the sake of convincing those who do not know it, but for the sake of defending those that do.

—William Blake

Truth only reveals itself when one gives up all preconceived ideas.

—Shoseki

It is a terrible thing for a man to find out suddenly that all his life he has been speaking nothing but the truth.

—Oscar Wilde

Truth breeds hatred.

—Bias of Priene, *Maxims*

… Science and mathematics
Run parallel to reality, they symbolize it, they squint at it,
They never touch it: consider what an explosion
Would rock the bones of men into little white fragments and unsky the world

If any mind for a moment touch truth.

—Robinson Jeffers, "The Silent Shepherds," *The Beginning & the End*

When one has one's hand full of truth it is not always wise to open it.

—French Proverb

The truth will set you free, but first it will make you miserable.

—Jim Davis

There is no truth. There is only perception.

—Gustave Flaubert

If a thousand old beliefs were ruined in our march to truth we must still march on.

—Stopford Brooke

UNITY

You'll never get mixed up if you simply tell the truth. Then you don't have to remember what you have said, and you never forget what you have said.

—Representative Sam Rayburn

Somebody said that it couldn't be done,
But he with a chuckle replied
That "maybe it couldn't" but he would be one
Who wouldn't say so till he'd tried.
So he buckled right in with the trace of a grin
On his face. If he worried he hid it.
He started to sing as he tackled the thing
That couldn't be done, and he did it.

—Edgar A. Guest

... It is common sense to take a method and try it; if it fails, admit it frankly and try another. But above all, try something. The millions who are in want will not stand by silently forever while the things to satisfy their needs are within easy reach.

—Franklin D. Roosevelt

Civilisation will not last, freedom will not survive, peace will not be kept, unless a very large majority of mankind unite together to defend them and show themselves possessed of a constabulary power before which barbaric and atavistic forces will stand in awe.

—Winston Churchill

All for one, one for all, that is our device, is it not?

—Alexandre Dumas

We cannot stand still or slip backwards. We must go forward now together.

—Gerald R. Ford

We must all hang together, or most assuredly we shall all hang separately.

—Attributed to Benjamin Franklin

For the strength of the Pack is the Wolf, and the strength of the Wolf is the Pack.

—Rudyard Kipling

Behold, how good and how pleasant it is for brethren to dwell together in unity!

—Psalms 133:1—2.

And see the confluence of dreams
That clashed together in our night,
One river born of many streams

Roll in one blaze of blinding light!

—George William Russell

VICTORY

God how the dead men
Grin by the wall,
Watching the fun
Of the Victory Ball,

—Alfred Noyes, *A Victory Dance*

Woe to the vanquishedl
(Vae victisi)

—Plautus, *Pseudolus*

Another such victory over the Romans, and we are undone.

—Pyrrhus (in Plutarch's *Lives*)

"But what good came of it at last?"
guoth little Peterkin.
"Why that I cannot tell," said he
"But't was a famous victory."

—Southey, *The Battle of Blenheim*

Nothing except a battle lost can be half so melancholy as a battle won.

—Duke Of Wellington, *Dispatch* 1815

The people who remained victorious were less like conquerors than conquered.

—St. Augustine

You ask, what is our aim? I can answer in one word: It is victory, victory at all costs, victory in spite of all terror, victory, however long and hard the road may be; for without victory, there is no survival.

—Winston Churchill

No retreat. No retreat. They must conquer or die who've no retreat.

—John Gay

There's an old saying that victory has 100 fathers and defeat is an orphan.

—John F. Kennedy

Beware of rashness, but with energy, and sleepless vigilance, go forward and give us victories.

—Abraham Lincoln

Upon the fields of friendly strife
Are sown the seeds
That, upon other fields, on other days
Will bear the fruits of victory.

—General Douglas Macarthur

Be ashamed to die until you have won some victory for humanity.

—Horace Mann

WAR

When civil dudgeon first grew high,
And men fell out, they knew not why;
When hard words, jealousies and fears,
Set folks together by the ears,
And made them fight, like mad or drunk,
For dame Religion as for punk; ...

—Butler, *Hudibras* (opening lines)

The Assyrian came down like the wolf on the fold,
And his cohorts were gleaming in purple and gold;
And the sheen of their spears was like stars on the sea,
When the blue waves roll nightly on deep Galilee.

—Byron, *The Destruction of Sennacherib*

And 'mid the tumult Kubla heard from far
Ancestral voices prophesying war.

—S. T. Coleridge, *Kubla Khan*

By the rude bridge that arched the flood,
Their flag to April's breeze unfurled,
Here once the embattled farmers stood,
And fired the shot heard round the world.

—Emerson, *Concord Hymn*

Yes; quaint and curious war is!
You shoot a fellow down
You'd treat if met where any bar is,
Or help to half—a—crown.

—Thomas Hardy, *The Man He Killed*

They wrote in the old days that it Is sweet and fitting to die for one's country. But in modern war there is nothing sweet nor fitting In your dying. You will die like a dog for no good reason,

—Ernest Hemingway, *Notes on the Next War*

The tumult and the shouting dies,
The captains and the kings depart.

—Kipling, *The Recessional*

Doughboys were paid a whole dollar a day
and received free burial under the clay.
And movie heroes are paid even more
shooting one another in a Hollywood war.

—Kreymborg, *What Price Glory*

There was laughter and loving In the lanes at evening;
Handsome were the boys then, and girls were gay."
But lost in Flanders by medalled commanders
The lads of the village are vanished away.

—Cecil Day Lewis, A *Time to Dance*

Ez fer war, I call it murder,—
There you hev it plain an' flat;
I don't want to go no furder
Than my Testyment fer that;
God hez said so plump an' fairly,'
It's ez long ez it Is broad,
An' you've gut to git up airly
Ef you want to take in God.

—J. R. Lowell, *The Biglow Papers, II*

War should be the only study of a prince. He should consider peace only as a breathing-time, which gives him leisure to contrive, and furnishes as ability to execute, military plans,

—Macchiavelli, *The Prince*

War alone keys up all human energies to their maximum tension and sets the seal of nobility on those peoples who have the courage to face it.

—Benito Mussolini, *Fascism*

I still remember the effect I produced on a small group of Galla tribesmen massed around a man in black clothes, I dropped an aerial torpedo right in the center, and the group opened up like a flowering rose, It was most entertaining.

—Vittorio Mussolini, In an account of his Ethiopian fighting

... and he smelleth the battle afar off, the thunder of the captains, and the shouting.

—Old Testament, Job, *XXXIX,* 25

They shall not pass.
(*Ils ne passeront pas*)

—General Petain (1916)

Stand! the ground's your own, my braves!
Will ye give it up to slaves?

—John Pierpont, *Warren's Address*

From the Rio Crande's waters to the icy lakes of Maine,
Let all exult, for we have met the enemy again,
Beneath their stern old mountains we have met them in their pride,
And rolled from Buena Vista back the battle's bloody tide.

—Gen. Albert Pike, *The Battle of Buena Vista*

The terrible rumble, grumble and roar
Telling the battle was on once more—
And Sheridan twenty miles away!

—T. B. Read, *Sheridan's Ride*

The American people will not relish the idea of any American citizen growing rich and fat in an emergency of blood and slaughter and human suffering.

—Franklin D. Roosevelt, Radio chat, May, 1940

In order for a war to be just, three things are necessary. First, the authority of the sovereign ... Secondly, a just cause ... Thirdly a rightful intention.

—St. Thomas Aquinas

Croesus said to Cambyses; That peace was better than war; because in peace the sons did bury their fathers, but in wars the fathers did bury their sons.

—Francis Bacon

The eagle has ceased to scream, but the parrots will now begin to chatter. The war of the giants is over and the pigmies will now start to squabble.

—Winston Churchill

War is not merely a political act but a real political instrument, a continuation of political intercourse, a carrying out of the same by other means.

—Karl Von Clausewitz

... war is nothing but a continuation of political intercourse with an admixture of other means.

—Karl von Clausewitz

I say when you get into a war, you should win as quick as you can, because your losses become a function of the duration of the war. I believe when you get in a war, get everything you need and win it.

—Dwight D. Eisenhowe

Nations have recently been led to borrow billions for war; no nation has ever borrowed largely for education. Probably, no nation is rich enough to pay for both war and civilization. We must make our choice; we cannot have both.

—Abraham Flexner

All of us who served in one war or another know very well that all wars are the glory and the agony of the young.

—Gerald R. Ford

Older men declare war. But it is youth that must fight and die. And it is youth who must inherit the tribulation, the sorrow and the triumphs that are the aftermath of war.

—Herbert Hoover

Among the calamities of war, may be justly numbered the diminution of the love of truth, by the falsehoods which interest dictates, and credulity encourages.

—Samuel Johnson

War is itself a political act with primarily political objects and under the American form of government political officials must necessarily direct its general course.

—Captain Dudley W. Knox

Once blood is shed in a national quarrel reason and right are swept aside by the rage of angry men.

—David Lloyd George

That's the way it is in war. You win or lose, live or die—and the difference is just an eyelash.

—Douglas Macarthur

War contains so much folly, as well as wickedness, that much is to be hoped from the progress of reason; and if any thing is to be hoped, every thing ought to be tried.

—James Madison

The enemy advances, we retreat; the enemy camps, we harass; the enemy tires, we attack; the enemy retreats, we pursue.

—Mao Tse-Tung

War is an ugly thing, but not the ugliest of things: the decayed and degraded state of moral and patriotic feeling which thinks nothing worth a war, is worse.

—John Stuart Mill

War challenges virtually every other institution of society—the justice and equity of its economy, the adequacy of its political systems, the energy of its productive plant, the bases, wisdom and purposes of its foreign policy.

—Walter Millis

Stand your ground. Don't fire unless fired upon, but if they mean to have a war, let it begin here.

—John Parker

I have always said that a conference was held for one reason only, to give everybody a chance to get sore at everybody else. Sometimes it takes two or three conferences to scare up a war, but generally one will do it.

—Will Rogers

Wars are, of course, as a rule to be avoided; but they are far better than certain kinds of peace.

—Theodore Roosevelt

Be convinced that to be happy means to be free and that to be free means to be brave. Therefore do not take lightly the perils of war.

—Thucydides

A time will come when a. politician who has wilfully made war and promoted international dissension will be as sure of the dock and much surer of the noose than a private homicide. It is not reasonable that those who gamble with men's lives should not stake their own.

—H. G. Wells

WOMEN

Rich widows are the only secondhand goods that sell at first-class prices.

—Attributed to Benjamin Franklin

An incautious congressman playfully ran his hand over Nick's shiny scalp and commented, "It feels just like my wife's backside." Nick instantly repeated the gesture. "So it does," he replied.

—Nicholas Longworth

A man likes his wife to be just clever enough to comprehend his cleverness, and just stupid enough to admire it.

—Israel Zangwill

If perticuliar care and attention is not paid to the Ladies we are determined to foment a Rebelion, and will not hold ourselves bound by any Laws in which we have no voice, or Representation.

—Abigail Adams

Next to God, we are indebted to women, first for life itself, and then for making it worth having.

—C. Nestell Bovee

On one issue, at least, men and women agree: they both distrust women.

—H. L. Mencken

Patience makes a woman beautiful in middle age.

—Attributed to Ellior Paul

One should never trust a woman who tells one her real age. A woman who would tell one that would tell one anything.

—Oscar Wilde

If a woman has to choose between catching a fly ball and saving an infant's life, she will choose to save the infant's life without even considering if there are men on base.

—Dave Barry

Women like silent men. They think they're listening.

—Marcel Achard, *Quote*, 4 November 1956

Sure God created man before woman. But then you always make a rough draft before the final masterpiece.

—Author Unknown

Some men know that a light touch of the tongue, running from a woman's toes to her ears, lingering in the softest way possible in various places in between, given often enough and sincerely enough, would add immeasurably to world peace.

—Marianne Williamson, "*A Woman's Worth*"

Women cannot complain about men anymore until they start getting better taste in them.

—Bill Maher

A male gynecologist is like an auto mechanic who has never owned a car.

—Carrie Snow

You start out happy that you have no hips or boobs. All of a sudden you get them, and it feels sloppy. Then just when you start liking them, they start drooping.

—Cindy Crawford

Every girl should use what Mother Nature gave her before Father Time takes it away.

—Laurence J. Peter

The average woman would rather have beauty than brains, because the average man can see better than he can think.

—Author Unknown

A woman can say more in a sigh than a man can say in a sermon.

—Arnold Haultain

Whatever women do they must do twice as well as men to be thought half as good. Luckily, this is not difficult.

—Charlotte Whitton

The two women exchanged the kind of glance women use when no knife is handy.

—Ellery Queen

Curve: The loveliest distance between two points.

—Mae West

Can you imagine a world without men? No crime and lots of happy fat women.

—Nicole Hollander

Women get the last word in every argument. Anything a man says after that is the beginning of a new argument.

—Author Unknown

Next to the wound, what women make best is the bandage.

—Jules Barbey d'Aurevilly

The rarest thing in the world is a woman who is pleased with photographs of herself.

—Elizabeth Metcalf

A man's face is his autobiography. A woman's face is her work of fiction.

—Oscar Wilde

There's something luxurious about having a girl light your cigarette. In fact, I got married once on account of that.

—Harold Robbins

The most popular image of the female despite the exigencies of the clothing trade is all boobs and buttocks, a hallucinating sequence of parabolae and bulges.

—Germaine Greer

Whether they give or refuse, it delights women just the same to have been asked.

—Ovid

Howiver, I'm not denyin' the women are foolish: God Almighty made 'em to match the men.

—George Eliot, "The Harvest Supper," *Adam Bede*

Women are like elephants to me. I like to look at them, but I wouldn't want to own one.

—W.C. Fields

Women really do rule the world. They just haven't figured it out yet. When they do, and they will, we're all in big big trouble.

—"Doctor" Leon of drleons.com

Ah, women. They make the highs higher and the lows more frequent.

—Author Unknown

I expect Woman will be the last thing civilized by Man.

—George Meredith

Men who don't like girls with brains don't like girls.

—Mignon McLaughlin, *The Second Neurotic's Notebook*, 1966

Women keep a special corner of their hearts for sins they have never committed.

—Cornelia Otis Skinner

Lovely female shapes are terrible complicators of the difficulties and dangers of this earthly life, especially for their owners.

—George du Maurier

Every woman is wrong until she cries, and then she is right — instantly.

—Sam Slick (Thomas Chandler Haliburton)

Men have been trained and conditioned by women, not unlike the way Pavlov conditioned his dogs, into becoming their slaves. As compensation for their labours men are given periodic use of a woman's vagina.

—Esther Vilar

The essence of life is the smile of round female bottoms, under the shadow of cosmic boredom.

—Guy de Maupassant

I have an idea that the phrase "weaker sex" was coined by some woman to disarm some man she was preparing to overwhelm.

—Ogden Nash

When men reach their sixties and retire, they go to pieces. Women go right on cooking.

—Gail Sheehy

The torment that so many young women know, bound hand and foot by love and motherhood, without having forgotten their former dreams.

—Simone de Beauvoir

They call it PMS because Mad Cow Disease was already taken.

—Author Unknown

Be to her virtues very kind,
Be to her faults a little blind.

—Matthew Prior

They may talk of a comet, or a burning mountain, or some such bagatelle; but to me a modest woman, dressed out in all her finery, is the most tremendous object of the whole creation.

—Oliver Goldsmith

A highbrow is a man who has found something more interesting than women.

—Edgar Wallace

It upsets women to be, or not to be, stared at hungrily.

—Mignon McLaughlin, *The Neurotic's Notebook*, 1960

You see, dear, it is not true that woman was made from man's rib; she was really made from his funny bone.

—J.M. Barrie, *What Every Woman Knows*

If women didn't exist, all the money in the world would have no meaning.

—Aristotle Onassis

Men will always delight in a woman whose voice is lined with velvet.

—Brendan Francis

Men really prefer reasonably attractive women; they go after the sensational ones to impress other men.

—Mignon McLaughlin, *The Second Neurotic's Notebook*, 1966

I married beneath me — all women do.

—Nancy Astor, speech, Oldham, England, 1951

Women are never stronger than when they arm themselves with their weakness.

—Marie de Vichy—Chamrond, Marquise du Deffand, *Letters to Voltaire*

Women dress alike all over the world: they dress to be annoying to other women.

—Elsa Schiaparelli

If President Nixon's secretary, Rosemary Woods, had been Moses' secretary, there would only be eight commandments.

—Art Buchwald, 1974

Woman begins by resisting a man's advances and ends by blocking his retreat.

—Oscar Wilde

She wore a short skirt and a tight sweater and her figure described a set of parabolas that could cause cardiac arrest in a yak.

—Woody Allen, *Getting Even*, 1973

It is only rarely that one can see in a little boy the promise of a man, but one can almost always see in a little girl the threat of a woman.

—Alexandre Dumas

I'd rather have two girls at seventeen than one at thirty—four.

—Fred Allen

When a woman comes to her glass, she does not employ her time in making herself look more advantageously what she really is, but endeavours to be as much another creature as she possibly can. Whether this happens because they stay so long and attend their work so diligently that they forget the faces and persons which they first sat down with, or whatever it is, they seldom rise from the toilet the same woman they appeared when they began to dress.

—Joseph Addison

All women are basically in competition with each other for a handful of eligible men.

—Mignon McLaughlin, *The Second Neurotic's Notebook*, 1966

A woman should soften but not weaken a man.

—Sigmund Freud

Women are in league with each other, a secret conspiracy of hearts and pheromones.

—Camille Paglia

When I glimpse the backs of women's knees I seem to hear the first movement of Beethoven's *Pastoral Symphony*.

—Author Unknown

No woman wants to see herself too clearly.

—Mignon McLaughlin, *The Second Neurotic's Notebook*, 1966

I prefer the word homemaker, because housewife always implies that there may be a wife some, place else.

—Bella Abzug

Women go to beauty parlours, for the unmussed look men hate.

—Mignon McLaughlin, *The Neurotic's Notebook*, 1960

Women polish the silver and water the plants and wait to be really needed.

—Mignon McLaughlin, *The Neurotic's Notebook*, 1960

The most beautiful make—up of a woman is passion. But cosmetics are easier to buy.

—Yves Saint Laurent

You have to have the kind of body that doesn't need a girdle in order to get to pose in one.

—Carolyn Kenmore

There are women who do not like to cause suffering to many men at a time, and who prefer to concentrate on one man: These are the faithful women.

—Alfred Capus

The same passions in man and woman nonetheless differ in tempo; hence man and woman do not cease misunderstanding one another.

—Friedrich Nietzsche, *Beyond Good and Evil*

Men enjoy being thought of as hunters, but are generally too lazy to hunt. Women, on the other hand, love to hunt, but would rather nobody knew it.

—Mignon McLaughlin, *The Second Neurotic's Notebook*, 1966

I've reached the age where competence is a turn-on.

—Billy Joel

You know, women always could endure more than men. Not only physically, but mentally — did you ever get a peek at some of the husbands?

—Will Rogers

[T]he first time Adam had a chance he laid the blame on woman.

—Nancy Astor, *My Two Countries*

God did it on purpose so that we may love you men instead of laughing at you.

—Mrs. Patrick Campbell, in reply to a male acquaintance who asked why women seem to have no sense of humor

Men at most differ as Heaven and Earth, but women, worst and best, as Heaven and Hell.

—Alfred Lord Tennyson

A woman asks little of love: only that she be able to feel like a heroine.

—Mignon McLaughlin, *The Second Neurotic's Notebook*, 1966

The chief excitement in a woman's life is spotting women who are fatter than she is.

—Helen Rowland

I would rather trust a woman's instinct than a man's reason.

—Stanley Baldwin

I should like to know what is the proper function of women, if it is not to make reasons for husbands to stay at home, and still stronger reasons for bachelors to go out.

—George Eliot, *The Mill on the Floss*

Men look *at* themselves in mirrors. Women look *for* themselves.

—Elissa Melamed

If your husband expects you to laugh, do so; if he expects you to cry, don't; if you don't know what he expects, what are you doing married?

—Mignon McLaughlin, *The Second Neurotic's Notebook*, 1966

I do not spoil women ... I don't send them flowers and gifts ... I am saving those gestures until I am an unpleasant old man who must resort to bribery to win a woman's synthetic affections.

—George Sanders

Women do not find it difficult nowadays to behave like men, but they often find it extremely difficult to behave like gentlemen.

—Compton Mackenzie, *Literature in My Time*, 1933

Let us leave the beautiful women to men with no imagination.

—Marcel Proust, *Albertine disparue*, 1925

Women deserve to have more than twelve years between the ages of twenty—eight and forty.

—James Thurber, *Time*, 15 August 1960

Dramatic art in her opinion is knowing how to fill a sweater.

—Bette Davis, about Jayne Mansfield

A woman's whole life is a history of the affections.

—Washington Irving

Women who make men talk better than they are accustomed to are always popular.

—E.V. Lucas

I'm not against half naked girls — not as often as I'd like to be.

—Benny Hill

You should never say anything to a woman that even remotely suggests that you think she's pregnant unless you can see an actual baby emerging from her at that moment.

—Dave Barry, "Things That It Took Me 50 Years to Learn"

The supply of good women far exceeds that of the men who deserve them.

—Robert Graves

What men desire is a virgin who is a whore.

—Edward Dahlbert

Women are afraid of mice and of murder, and of very little in between.

—Mignon McLaughlin, *The Second Neurotic's Notebook*, 1966

A woman should be an illusion.

—Ian Fleming

It is because of men that women dislike one another.

—Jean de La Bruyère, *Characters*, 1688

If you are ever in doubt as to whether to kiss a pretty girl, always give her the benefit of the doubt.

—Thomas Carlyle

Women who feel naked without their lipstick are well over thirty.

—Mignon McLaughlin, *The Second Neurotic's Notebook*, 1966

Women are like dogs really. They love like dogs, a little insistently. And they like to fetch and carry and come back wistfully after hard words, and learn rather easily to carry a basket.

—Mary Roberts Rinehart

It's the good girls who keep the diaries; the bad girls never have the time.

—Tallulah Bankhead

A husband only worries about a particular Other Man; a wife distrusts her whole species.

—Mignon McLaughlin, *The Second Neurotic's Notebook*, 1966

I believe you should place a woman on a pedestal, high enough so you can look up her dress.

—Steve Martin

A woman who cannot be ugly is not beautiful.

—Karl Kraus

A man chases a woman until she catches him.

—American Proverb

Variability is one of the virtues of a woman. It avoids the crude requirement of polygamy. So long as you have one good wife you are sure to have a spiritual harem.

—G.K. Chesterton, *Alarms and Discursions*, 1910

Brains are an asset, if you hide them.

—Mae West

With men, as with women, the main struggle is between vanity and comfort; but with men, comfort often wins.

—Mignon McLaughlin, *The Second Neurotic's Notebook*, 1966

Once a woman has given you her heart, you can never get rid of the rest of her.

—John Vanbrugh, *The Relapse*, 1696

Is it too much to ask that women be spared the daily struggle for superhuman beauty in order to offer it to the caresses of a subhumanly ugly mate?

—Germaine Greer, *The Female Eunuch*, 1970

A woman can look both moral and exciting … if she also looks as if it was quite a struggle.

—Edna Ferber

Women have very little idea of how much men hate them.

—Germaine Greer

Do you not know I am a woman? When I think, I must speak.

—William Shakespeare, *As You Like It*

Being a woman is of special interest only to aspiring male transsexuals. To actual women, it is simply a good excuse not to play football.

—Fran Lebowitz

You're booty blinded. You know what that is? It's like being snowblinded only it ain't no snow, it's a cute little piece of ass.

—From the movie *I Spy*

Women are never landlocked: they're always mere minutes away from the briny deep of tears.

—Mignon McLaughlin, *The Second Neurotic's Notebook*, 1966

To get to a woman's heart, a man must first use his own.

—Mike Dobbertin, quoted in *A 5th Portion of Chicken Soup for the Soul*

Woman's virtue is man's greatest invention.

—Cornelia Otis Skinner

Nature has given women so much power, that the law has very wisely given them little.

—Samuel Johnson

Women speak two languages — one of which is verbal.

—William Shakespeare

Women are wiser than men, because they know less and understand more.

—James Thurber

I hate women, because they always know where things are.

—Voltaire

Good-looking girls break hearts, and goodhearted girls mend them.

—Mignon McLaughlin, *The Second Neurotic's Notebook*, 1966

Fighting is essentially a masculine idea; a woman's weapon is her tongue.

—Hermione Gingold

The people I'm furious with are the women's liberationists. They keep getting up on soapboxes and proclaiming women are brighter than men. That's true, but it should be kept quiet or it ruins the whole racket.

—Anita Loos, *New York Times*, 10 February 1974

Women always worry about the things that men forget; men always worry about the things women remember.

—Author Unknown

No matter how happily a woman may be married, it always pleases her to discover that there is a nice man who wishes that she were not.

—H.L. Mencken